THE
HAMPTONS
KITCHEN

THE
HAMPTONS
KITCHEN

SEASONAL RECIPES PAIRING LAND AND SEA

HILLARY DAVIS *and* **STACY DERMONT**

INCLUDING ORIGINAL PHOTOGRAPHY
BY BARBARA LASSEN

FOREWORD BY GAEL GREENE

THE COUNTRYMAN PRESS
A division of W. W. Norton & Company
Independent Publishers Since 1923

Photo Credits: pages 22–23: © ediebloom/iStockPhoto.com; page 25: ©wmaster890/iStockPhoto.com; page 28: © Shaiith/iStockPhoto.com; page 31: © Selwa Baroody/iStockPhoto.com; page 59: © hofack2/iStockPhoto.com; page 63: © izhairguns/iStockPhoto.com; page 64–65: © yellowsarah/iStockPhoto.com; page 67: © Nikolay_Donetsk/iStockPhoto.com; page 77: © PhotoAllel/iStockPhoto.com; page 87: © margouillatphotos/iStockPhoto.com; page 98–99: © ediebloom/iStockPhoto.com; page 105: © hofack2/iStockPhoto.com; page 117: © fotostorm/iStockPhoto.com; page 130: © Nataliia Sirobaba/iStockPhoto.com; page 148–49: © Lubo Ivanko/iStockPhoto.com; page 162: © stephconnell/iStockPhoto.com; page 169: © DipaliS/iStockPhoto.com; page 185: © bhofack2/iStockPhoto.com; page 190–91: © Alinakho/iStockPhoto.com; page 214: © Mariha-kitchen/iStockPhoto.com; page 219: © zeleno/iStockPhoto.com

CONTENTS

FOREWORD BY GAEL GREENE: TASTY MEMORIES

My adored husband and I had separated. There didn't seem to be much choice. He was in love with her, he said. I had a fall deadline for the first third of my novel. I would find a house in the Hamptons and force myself to write.

I always longed for the beach. But Don had preferred the country. That's why we bought the little church on top of the hill outside Woodstock. The one consolation of seeing my life fall apart was, now, at last I could go to the beach.

My Hamptons—Bridgehampton, Wainscott, Amagansett—has always been about food. What will we cook? Who do we know that can get us into Nick & Toni's or the season's torrid new spot (that most probably won't be around by next year).

I didn't swim. I'd never surf. I had no interest in boating or fishing. I am a most unlikely beach person. But I love it. That first sad and uncertain summer, I moved into Dan and Rita Wynn's weathered gray cedar house in Springs not far from Craig Claiborne's place. One day I was pretending to swim, when a car full of Frenchmen arrived and took over Craig's kitchen. They had come to cook the buffet lunch for the wedding of Pierre Franey's oldest daughter.

The new young chef de cuisine of Le Cirque seemed shy. I teased him for not putting on shorts like the others. But that's another story.

This book is a love affair with seaside eating. Each new summer I would promise to live on vegetables and fish and shed the pounds I'd gained reviewing restaurants all year. But in that first year on Bay Lane I discovered Devon Fredericks's Loaves and Fishes on Sagg Main and every weekend I would buy her sour cream coffee cake and maybe an extra, just in case.

Devon doesn't recall where she and her partner got the recipe, but she remembers going with me to Silver's for lunch in Southampton so that I could dissect the experience for an early restaurant roundup. (Devon is married to Eli Zabar now, more evidence that romance in the Hamptons starts with food.)

Most days I would find a quiet spot on the beach for my old blanket and, masked in sunscreen under a big hat, I would read novels and think about dinner. For me the Hamptons was often about cooking with friends on the weekend. I found an enthusiastic coconspirator in Harley Baldwin, who would, a few years later, focus his real estate and social creativity on the Caribou Club empire in Aspen.

But long before Aspen, Harley would visit on weekends. I would chop raw clams and bake them in the shell under peppery crumbs. There were always big, sun-ripened tomatoes, bursting with juice and painted with olive oil and dribbles of balsamic vinegar.

One Friday night Harley stopped at The Seafood Shop in Wainscott on the way to my rental of the year and arrived with an eight-pound lobster. It jumped out of the big brown bag.

"It's going to be tough," I promised him. He persuaded me to call Pierre Franey for advice on how long to steam it. "Eight pounds." Pierre laughed. I tied a blue ribbon around the critter's neck and walked him across the kitchen.

"The water's ready," Harley said. I closed the door and left the two of them to their final struggle. Much to my amazement, the lobster's torso was perfectly tender. Perhaps, it was Pierre's blessing.

One foggy afternoon of another summer escape, I stood in front of my A-frame and watched a lone fisherman pulling in bluefish. He offered to clean a really big one for me. I took it into the kitchen, and then

thought . . . now what? Would I ever have a fresher fish? I called Pierre Franey and asked him what to do with it. He offered to come by and cook it for me.

He looked around my kitchen. He found some olive oil and some mustard and made mayonnaise. I didn't have much to work with except too many overripe tomatoes. He dropped them in boiling water to peel them quickly and smashed them, sprinkled a bit of onion and garlic sautéed in butter and lay two big fillets of fish on top. Then he painted them with the mayo. A few minutes in the oven, then a quick binge under the broiler.

I poured some icy wine from the fridge and toasted Pierre. Many people don't like bluefish, but all its flaws disappeared that evening in Pierre's alchemy. I cannot count the times since that I have mounted fish on smashed tomatoes and painted it with mayo. Hellmann's, of course.

About this book. In 2011, I did a dinner-and-reading to promote my memoir *Insatiable* at Eric Lemonides's Almond Restaurant in Bridgehampton. At the end,

Stacy Dermont emerged from a far corner. She had a basket filled with jars of preserves made from her garden fruit and a peach pie balanced on top—a gift for me. I knew her from her many food-related tales and gossip column in *Dan's Papers* and from interviews.

When I found myself booked on the Jitney for a desperately needed Hamptons getaway with my promised guest room suddenly not free, Stacy thought her new friend, Hillary Davis, might take me in—"Did I know Hillary's spectacularly beautiful French cookbooks?"

I moved into a guest room overlooking the garden with Hillary and her most agreeable guy. I brought them a pie from Round Swamp Farm and when I found it the next morning untouched on the kitchen counter, I demonstrated the joy of pie for breakfast by cutting the first piece for myself.

Yes, I was the one who insisted that Stacy and Hillary should put together the book that would be an irresistible celebration of the Hamptons for those of us who love to eat and drink and cook. And here it is.

—Gael Greene

INTRODUCTION

A white Range Rover was parked near the Tiffany-blue pool. I was in the Hamptons for the weekend, a place I had never visited. Once unpacked, I passed the Range Rover and began a long walk down the road toward the ocean beach. And this was when I realized there were two Hamptons. The one with the Tiffany-blue pool surrounded by a buzz-cut tall hedge, and the one I was passing on my walk, the one with a rickety farm stand at the side of a potato field.

Much like the French Riviera where I had lived for over 11 years, this was what is often referred to as America's Riviera, a magnet for the rich and famous. Jackson Pollock lived here; Marilyn Monroe and Arthur Miller loved here; Truman Capote wrote here; Ralph Lauren created here; Christie Brinkley and Alec Baldwin live here, as do a host of sophisticated world travelers and captains of industry. And like the French Riviera, the not-so-famous live here, the farmers, journalists, florists, doctors, chefs, commercial fishermen, struggling artists, would-be novelists, shop owners, and so many others that make it their year-round home.

These two Rivieras are also known for their food cultures, their artist colonies, and their vineyards. Both are famous destinations—places people come to in order to holiday in the sun, laze on the beach, spend quality family time, and invite friends to celebrate the good life.

And so, I came to live here. I continued to write cookbooks, and I also began a career as a real estate agent with Sotheby's in Bridgehampton. I was now not only living the dream but helping others find it as well. The Hamptons is filled with fabulous homes with Instagrammable kitchens and gardens, so it was a natural choice.

The move was a seamless transition, because both Rivieras are so alike: country living close to the sea. I reveled in discoveries of wonderful local produce and continued to bring people home with me to dine and to talk. Whether it is behind the hedges of a grand waterfront estate or at a spur-of-the-moment picnic on the beach, people come together here for food and friendship.

Stacy, my coauthor, was one of the first friends I made, and she continues to this day to be my closest. Food brought us together, and thereafter, friendship blossomed. Over many meals and food-oriented adventures, we came to the conclusion that we wanted to share what we love about this very special part of the world. We thought, as we discussed it, that as a team we were ultimately qualified to write a definitive cookbook for the Hamptons, not only because of our individual knowledge, but because as a team we represented the two sides of the Hamptons.

Stacy is the farm girl, the recognized expert in local produce and wines. Her cooking style and approach are totally in tune with our farm culture and history. It's authentically American. It's farm stand and farmers' market cuisine at its very best.

I, on the other side, have a background in French cooking that I love to translate using local ingredients, emphasizing color and style in recipes. I have written four French cookbooks from my experiences and knowledge gained in France. When I lived in Paris and in the south of France, it allowed me to travel all over that beautiful country. I tasted every pastry, pâté, and *poulet* I could each day. In my village in the south of France, I learned from neighbors how to cook the local cuisine that exists around the town of Nice, and later passed that knowledge on, giving cooking classes to expats living along the Riviera. The writing of French cookbooks followed.

So, Stacy represents the authentic and traditional farm-culture cuisine of this beautiful place. And I, perhaps, represent all the people who come to live here from other countries or other parts of America, from different lifestyles and cultures, from different backgrounds, who like me, now call this place home, and who are all drawn here for the same reasons.

We come here to flee a city or a hectic life, to be closer to nature, where we can have a garden and maybe learn how to cook from it, where we can hitch up our pants and go clamming or cast a rod into the surf, where we can hear the laughter of our kids running blindly in a corn maze, where we can walk down the road in Bridgehampton in the morning, able to hear the wind whoosh under the wings of migrating water birds. All of this nurtures our awareness of the fragile beauty of our environment and reminds us to participate in preserving it.

In the way we have chosen to live, we shop at our local farm stands and farmers' markets for most or all of our fresh produce, as much to revel in the amazing quality and choice as to feel as if we are taking part in preserving our small-farm heritage. Gastronomy as a life force is alive and well here, feeding both soul and body, as artisanal food crafters, chefs, farmers, baymen, fishermen, vintners, and residents define

the way we eat, encouraging us to become more and more local-centric. Hand-formed cheeses, non-GMO wheat, small-batch beers, basement-cured sauerkraut and kimchi, hyper-local handmade spirits, unrefined hand-harvested sea salt, even my homemade harissa, are testament to our shared passion for connecting with where we live and using what is around us.

This is our unifying bond. And it is a bond we wish to share with you. Whether you live in the Hamptons or in a town in the Midwest or in a sprawling metropolis, we hope this book invites you to join us in celebrating the good life, one filled with joy, friends, great

food, and the peace and sanity that nature provides. We invite you to bring the Hamptons home. We invite you to bring local flavors home.

Within this cookbook you will find recipes from both of us that we cook in our own styles, using as many of our local ingredients as possible, while melding in the spices, culinary traditions, and techniques that we call our own. Wherever you are, start with the best local ingredients, then follow our recipes. Follow us to the Hamptons.

—Hillary Davis
HillaryDavis@me.com

ON WINE, BEER, AND GOOD SPIRITS

We invite you to enjoy delicious Long Island wines with our seasonal dishes to fully celebrate regionality. Following the old adage that "what grows together, goes together," we offer pairings of local pours for most of our dishes, drawing from the wealth of local options. We don't suggest that you pair every course of a meal with a different alcoholic beverage. Rather, we offer insights so that you may explore the bounty of Long Island's East End.

Beyond our recommendations are thousands more possible pairing options, drawing from Long Island wines alone. We also offer general guidelines for pairings in any region.

A pairing is an enhancement of the dining experience that basically works in one of two ways—it either amplifies the flavor and expression of a dish, or it provides a pleasant contrast. So, for example, while I suggest pairing Bridge Lane's almost buttery rosé to enhance the eggy complexity of Hillary's Mile High Crustless Vegetable Pie, I suggest that the creaminess of Hillary's Baked Stuffed Zucchini Blossoms calls for the acidity in Channing Daughters Winery Rosato di Sculpture Garden. You see, the "science" behind food and beverage pairings is personal preference.

I've found pairings that work well for us, and we invite you to explore and expand on our "hard work," one sip at a time. We encourage you to adventure through the world of pairings just as we invite you to adapt our recipes to your tastes and predilections. Above all, relax and enjoy the journey to your own "Hamptons place."

Wines have no seasons, though light wines prevail in warmer weather with the lighter diet, while denser, concentrated dishes pair best with denser, concentrated wines. Yet sometimes a rosé is just the thing to accompany a rich winter repast of seafood.

Vintages vary; we encourage you to come to Long Island and do some vertical tastings to see how, for instance, nine straight days of rain in October of 2005 affected that year's wines. But, a blend of 75 percent Merlot and 25 percent Cabernet Franc from the same winery's vineyards, for example, will undoubtedly go well with meaty dishes

New York State is one of the largest grape producers in the United States. In fact, it is third, behind California and Washington, in acreage and production. New York's wine regions are located in temperate zones, which include the Niagara Region, the Champlain Valley, the Finger Lakes Region, the Hudson Valley, and Long Island. So locally produced wines are available from New York's Atlantic coast to the shores of Lake Erie and Lake Ontario.

Long Island is unique among New York's wine regions; we enjoy a long growing season and our cool Atlantic breezes produce the highest quality fruit. Our climate allows grapes to fully ripen, reaching the perfect balance of flavor and aroma. Here, unlike upstate, producers are able to grow European red varietals including Merlot, Pinot Noir, and Cabernet Sauvignon, in addition to white vinifera grapes, including Chardonnay, Sauvignon Blanc, and Riesling. Our growers and winemakers also conduct delightful experiments with somewhat lesser-known grapes, such as the German Dornfelder and the Italian Friulano. In recent years, we've seen local production of remarkable Gewürztraminers and pétillant-naturels, or "pet-nats," wines that are naturally sparkling because they are bottled before their primary fermentation is complete.

While the Fingers Lakes Region produces the world-famous Rieslings of Dr. Konstantin Frank and Hermann J. Wiemer, many upstate New York

vineyards plant European hybrids. Some of the wines made from these crosses between vinifera and native American grapes have achieved acclaim, especially those from the Hudson Valley.

Similar to France's Brittany, Long Island juts way out into the ocean. But would I really dare to compare Long Island to France? Absolutely. After all, the Long Island wine region is located at almost the same latitude as the wine growing regions of France, Italy, and the Napa Valley.

Long Island's East End splits into two forks—North and South. The South Fork, better known as "the Hamptons," comprises the towns of Southampton and East Hampton, which in turn encompass many villages and hamlets. Paumanok, which means "land of tribute," is a Native American name for Long Island.

This name refers to the prized purple quahog shells that were abundant along our shores. The shells were carved and drilled to make beads, known as wampum. Though used in trade and as currency by colonists, into the 1660s, wampum was more sacred in nature to the Native Americans, hence its use in making pictographic belts to commemorate important events.

At the cleft of land where the forks split is the town of Riverhead. Between these forks, or "the fish's tail," as Native Americans called Long Island's East End, lies Shelter Island, out in the Peconic Bay. Water, lots of water, makes our world go round.

Long Island is surrounded by the Atlantic Ocean, yet sheltered by both the Long Island Sound and the Peconic Bay. So, these large bodies of water and our rich soils influence the quality and character of our grapes, and hence, our wines. Our unique terroir was recognized by two separate American Viticultural Area designations in the 1980s—the North Fork AVA (which includes Shelter Island) and the Hamptons AVA, the South Fork. In 2001, the Long Island AVA, which takes in all of Long Island and its smaller islands, was established.

Alex and Louisa Hargrave planted Long Island's first commercial vineyard in 1973 in Cutchogue, which is on the North Fork. Today there are over 60 wineries across Long Island.

The North Fork is a bit drier and often a few degrees warmer than the South Fork. Its growing season for popular crops, including strawberries and corn, can run a full two weeks ahead of its southern neighbor. So, the South Fork often "imports" produce from the North Fork just ahead of its own fruit and vegetable seasons. Wine grapes are "brought down" annually to the South Fork. Some of our local wineries also now buy additional grapes from upstate New York and from as far away as South America to meet demand. But all the wines I suggest pairing with the dishes in this cookbook are Long Island grown. We feel that these wines naturally pair best with the fruits of our local *merroir* (food-growing water environs) and farms.

After almost 50 years of experimentation with our microclimates, Long Island Wine Country has come

of age—and the proof is in the bottles. If you try the many wines that I recommend, we're certain that you'll agree.

And then there are our local beers, liquors, and meads. Where to begin? With our water, of course. Long Islanders enjoy fresh drinking water from a sole-source aquifer. Much like the rich soil of Long Island, the underlying aquifer system was created in the last Ice Age by the passing of massive glaciers. The layered aquifers below our homes are the Upper Glacial, the Magothy, and the Lloyd aquifers. Below the Lloyd is bedrock.

Clean, unadulterated water is the best possible start for brewing beer. The talents of our local beer makers are increasingly enhanced by locally grown grains and hops.

In 2014, New York Governor Andrew Cuomo signed the Craft New York Act, which eased restrictions on craft beer producers, as well as small-scale distilleries and cideries. Cuomo accompanied that law with a bevy of grants in order to promote small-scale farming while increasing tax revenues. Today, more than 40 craft breweries operate on Long Island. And some of our growers of apples, grains, and potatoes are bottling the essence of this unique place. We raise a glass to them all!

—Stacy Dermont
StacyDermont.com

WHAT'S IN SEASON

Our wish to introduce you to the ingredients found in the Hamptons, and the recipes that showcase them, springs from the abundance of wonderful local produce and products that our farmers, fishermen, and winemakers offer for consumption.

The surf, sun, and vineyards of the Hamptons welcome visitors who increase our population tenfold every summer. The pervading party atmosphere means that our seasons are defined by celebrations as much as they are by the weather.

Year-Round

Many local products are now available year-round due to advances in storage, the use of hoophouses, and a warming climate. Year-round local produce and products include apples, arugula, beets, carrots, chard, cheese, cider, clams, cornmeal, daikon radishes, dried apples, dried beans, dried herbs, dried peppers, dried tomatoes, duck, eggs (though the egg supply drops considerably in the winter), ginger, honey, kale, kelp, maple syrup, meats, microgreens, mushrooms, oysters, parsley, potatoes, sea scallops, sprouts, turnips, and wheat berries. But because all plants have a peak season when they are most delicious and nutritious, you'll find some of these items listed by season.

Spring:
Easter/Passover to Memorial Day

Most of our spring crops are leaves or stalks, as fruits take more time to develop. Look for:

Asian greens, asparagus, baby greens, bamboo shoots, blue claw crab, bluefish, bok choy, broccoli rabe, chervil, chickweed, chives and chive blossoms, cilantro, collard greens, cress, dandelion greens and petals, fennel fronds, flounder (summer and winter), garlic chives, garlic mustard, green garlic, green onions, horseradish greens, hyssop, lamb's quarters, leeks, lemon balm, lemon verbena, lettuce, lovage, mackerel, marjoram, mint, mizuna, mustard flowers and greens, nasturtium leaves, oregano, parsley, parsnips, pea shoots, radishes, red raspberry leaves, rhubarb, sage, spinach, spring onions, squid, tatsoi, thyme, violet flowers, weakfish, and wild onions.

Other items that are not currently widely available on the East End in the springtime, but you may find at your local farmers' market, are fiddlehead ferns, morels, nettles, and ramps.

Low Summer:
Memorial Day to the Fourth of July

Many of our crops blossom in the early summer; others are in their immature, tender "baby" form. Look for:

Baby beets, baby cabbage, baby carrots, baby leeks, baby summer squash, bachelor button blooms, blowfish, blueberries, borage flowers, calendula blossoms, carrot greens, currants, early raspberries, fava beans, garlic scapes, grape leaves, Japanese turnips, mulberries, nasturtium blossoms, new potatoes, porgy, purslane, rosemary, scallions, shelling peas, snow peas, sour cherries, squash blossoms, strawberries, sugar snap peas, and turnips.

Still in season: Asian greens, asparagus, blue claw crab, bluefish, cilantro, collard greens, lettuces, mustard greens, radishes, rhubarb, spinach, summer flounder (a.k.a. fluke).

Some other items that are not currently widely available in the Hamptons in the early summer, but you may find at your local farmers' market, are elderberry flowers, Japanese knotweed shoots, sassafras leaves, and serviceberries.

High Summer: Fourth of July to Labor Day

Most of our fruits and many of our vegetables hit their peak in summer's heat. Look for:

Apricots, artichokes, Asian pears, basil, beach plums, beets, black currants, black raspberries, blackberries, broccolini, bush beans, butternut squash, cabbage, carrots, cauliflower, celery, chard, cherries, chokecherries, cucumbers, daikon radish, delicata squash, edamame, eggplant, elderberries, fennel, figs, garlic, ground cherries, kohlrabi, late peas, leeks, muskmelon, nectarines, onions, peaches, peppers, plums, potatoes, pumpkin leaves, red amaranth, red currants, shallots, snap beans, spaghetti squash, summer squash, sweet corn, tomatillos, tomatoes, turnips, watermelon, yellow raspberries, and zucchini.

Still in season: bachelor button blooms, blueberries, blue claw crab, calendula, cilantro, collard greens, porgy, purslane, raspberries, and squash blossoms.

Some other items that are not currently widely available in the Hamptons in the summertime, but you may find at your local farmers' market, are huckleberries, pluots, and sea rocket.

Fall: Labor Day to Thanksgiving

Fall tree fruits and squash that have been ripening for months reach their pinnacle, just in time to be harvested and stored for winter. Look for:

Apples, blackfish, broccoli, Brussels sprouts, celeriac, chicory, codfish, cranberries, fig leaves, ginger, gooseberries, hazelnuts, Jerusalem artichokes, kiwi berries, kousa dogwood cherries, late raspberries, pawpaws, pears, Peconic Bay scallops, pole beans, pumpkins, romanesco, turkey, turmeric, venison, wild grapes, and winter squash (acorn, buttercup, carnival, futsu, hubbard, kabocha, kuri, sweet dumpling).

Some cool-weather crops come back into season, including Asian greens, leeks, lettuces, radishes, scallions, and spinach. Collard greens just taste better in the spring and fall.

Still in season: beets, blue claw crab, butternut squash, cabbage, carrots, cauliflower, celery, cilantro, cucumbers, daikon radish, delicata squash, eggplant, fennel, garlic, ground cherries, honeynut squash, kohlrabi, onions, peppers, sweet corn, tomatillos, tomatoes, turnips, and watermelon.

And fall is the season of the biggest striped bass run off Long Island.

Some other items that are not currently widely available in the Hamptons in the fall, but you may find at your local farmers' market, are persimmons, fox grapes, and table grapes.

Winter: Thanksgiving to Easter/Passover

The hardiest of crops come into their own with the cold of winter. Look for:

Bok choy, burdock, endive, horseradish, kale, parsnips, and rutabaga.

Still in season: cabbage, celeriac, chickory, collard greens, onions, Peconic Bay scallops, porgy, and venison.

Though kales grow here year-round, they are much tastier after a hard frost, like all cruciferous vegetables. These include arugula, bok choy, broccoli, Brussels sprouts, cabbage, cauliflower, chards, kale, radish, rapini, rutabaga, spinach, sweet potatoes, turnip, and watercress. Root vegetables, including beets, carrots, leeks, onions, and parsnips, are sweeter after a hard frost, because in order to survive in the cold (to not freeze), some of their starches turn to sugars.

STOCKING THE HAMPTONS PANTRY

We use as many local products as possible, but some spices and other key ingredients just don't grow in the Hamptons. When we were brainstorming ideas for the best farmers' market-to-table cookbook we could imagine, we agreed that we'd have to include a few imports.

At the end of this chapter we include a list of the ingredients used in this cookbook that you won't likely find at a farmers' market in the Northeastern United States.

We suggest that you stock your pantry with them (though you probably have most of these ingredients in your home already) and then try to shop exclusively at your local farmers' market for a whole summer season before hitting the store again. You'll find that it's fun and rewarding to cook this way.

We also want to talk to you about fats and salt. They often get a bad rap, but both are absolutely necessary in the human diet.

Fats: We always use European-style butter. If you switch from American-style butter, you'll be sure to notice the huge difference in flavor that just a bit more fat and cultured tang makes. Most of our recipes call for unsalted butter because this makes for better flavor in the final product. It also gives you more control over how much salt the given dish contains.

We're thrilled to be able to purchase New York State–produced European-style butter from our local farmers' market and several local stores.

While Stacy often chooses to use grapeseed oil because it is a domestically produced, neutral oil with a high smoke point, Hillary almost always uses olive oil. Other oils used in our recipes include butternut squash, pumpkin, and sesame. Each has a uniquely distinct flavor and texture.

Salts: All salts are at least 97.5 percent pure sodium chloride. Between us, we've probably tried 97.5 percent of the thousands of salts in the world and we swear by our local Amagansett Sea Salt. Its slow-grown solar crystals and its tiny percentage of minerals, algae, and clay sets it apart. Hillary uses sea salt exclusively, while Stacy sometimes uses kosher salt. Kosher salt has a duller, rounder taste than sea salt and the fact that kosher salt is more uniform in shape and consistency can also be a factor in choosing it for some dishes. And it's less likely to stick to your fingers. Sometimes we call for a fine sea salt for a hint of the sea that also blends in quickly and thoroughly.

Sugar: When we refer to "sugar" in a recipe it is white, granulated sugar. Though derived from plants, it is not considered a vegan ingredient because bone char is typically used in its refining processes.

Flour: When we refer to "flour" in a recipe it is all-purpose wheat flour.

Vinegar: Neither of us generally use white vinegar because, in the United States, most of it is now made from corn.

Nonlocal ingredients used in this book: active dry yeast, balsamic vinegar, bay leaves, black onion seeds, chickpea-fava bean flour, chickpeas, chocolate, cinnamon, cocoa powder, coffee, cornstarch, cumin, Dijon mustard, double-acting baking powder, hazelnut extract, kosher salt, lemons, Midori, mirin, mustard seeds, nori, nutmeg, olives, oranges, paprika, Parmesan, Parmigiano-Reggiano, Pecorino Romano, pepper (black, pink, white), prosciutto, pure vanilla extract, rice, saffron, soy sauce, sugar, tea, vanilla beans, white balsamic vinegar, white chocolate, Worcestershire sauce.

NOTHING GOES TO WASTE

To do our part to help preserve our beautiful landscape, we re-use or compost many of our kitchen scraps. For our stock recipe, see page 230, and for our compost recipe, see page 233.

Here's a list of items featured in recipes in this book you may set aside for use in making stock:

- bones
- wing tips and other offcuts
- lobster shells
- allium trimmings = onions, leeks, shallots, garlic, chives
- trimmings from these herbs: parsley, lovage, marjoram, oregano, thyme
- mushroom stipes
- carrot greens
- pepper trimmings
- corn cobs
- celeriac trimmings

Here's a list of the kitchen scraps from recipes in this book that may be composted:

- vegetable trimmings
- fruit trimmings
- herb trimmings
- eggshells
- seeds
- small amounts of oil used to cook food
- leftover marinades
- cooking liquids
- pickling brine
- leftover juice
- corn husks
- melon rinds
- squash shells
- bamboo skewers
- used muffin papers
- used paper toweling
- used paper napkins
- paper bags used in food preparation
- coffee grounds (and paper filters)
- used tea bags
- used bay leaves
- used vanilla beans
- used cloves
- citrus rinds

Chapter One

SPRING

Easter/Passover to Memorial Day

Spring in the Hamptons signals the arrival of many
things green: peas, baby lettuces, asparagus, and herbs.
With them comes a shift in the local fishing stocks.
This chapter provides recipes using this bounty.

SMALL PLATES

Baguette with Radishes, Homemade Butter, and Sea Salt 24
Mashed Potato Flatbread Topped with Poached Egg 26
Asparagus Soup with Whipped Parmesan Cream 28
Green Garlic Pesto Bites 30

SALADS

Spring Onion and Arugula Salad with Yogurt Dressing 32
Hamptons Bamboo Shoots and Roasted Vegetable Bowl 35
Butter Lettuce and Asparagus Salad with Warm Mustard Leaf Vinaigrette 37

MAINS

Hamptons Fish Burger with Microgreens 38
Radish Greens Pesto over a Tangle of Pasta 40
Poached Cod and Clams in Buttered Broth 42
Spring Spatchcocked Chicken Pan Supper 46
Flounder Swimming in Merlot 48

DESSERTS

Strawberry Layer Cake with Rhubarb Jam Filling 52
Fresh Mint Ice Cream with Chocolate Sauce 55
Sweet Carrot Flan 56
Potato Cheesecake with Caramel Crust 58
Traditional Strawberry Shortcake 61

Baguette with Radishes, Homemade Butter, and Sea Salt

1 quart heavy whipping cream
1 bunch radishes
1 thin baguette, sliced diagonally into ¼- to ½-inch slices
Sea salt flakes to sprinkle (I prefer Maldon Sea Salt Flakes for this sandwich)
Fresh chives for garnish

Healthy radish greens may be used in making the Radish Greens Pesto over a Tangle of Pasta on page 40.

You can use the leftover whey from making the butter for baking, instead of milk.

There are few primary colors in the Hamptons. Gray-shingled houses with white trim almost match gray-shingled windmills. This is a watercolor place, washed in muted calming hues of golden sand, grays, and soft-dirt browns.

Color comes from the garden. Vibrant basil. Sunset-colored peppers. Sunrise-colored shucked corn. And ruby- and hot pink–colored radishes that intrigue and inspire me. I use them in this rustic, French, open-face tartine, a deceptively simple sandwich using the best ingredients: the highest quality butter, fresh tender young radishes, and sea salt flakes.

I make my own butter, which is simple and fun to do. Did anyone ever tell you, "Be careful whipping the cream! If you do it too long, it will turn into butter!" Right! That's how easy it is. One quart of cream will make a half pound of butter, and it takes mere minutes. *—Hillary*

SERVES 4

1. Put the cream into the bowl of a stand mixer and beat it on high. Once it has turned into whipped cream, drape a towel over the top of the mixer because, as you continue to beat it, it will, all of a sudden, begin to change into butter, and the whey water thrown off during this process can suddenly splash out of the bowl. You will know when it happens because you will hear a slapping sound. Stop and take a peek under the towel. You should see the butter sitting in a lot of liquid.

2. Scoop the butter out. Squeeze the butter together in your hands over the sink under cold running water to wash away any remaining whey. You can then wrap it in cheesecloth and squeeze it again over the sink. Unwrap the butter, and scoop it into an airtight container and refrigerate it until ready to use. For this recipe, leave it out to come to room temperature.

3. Wash, dry, then thinly slice the radishes.

4. Generously spread the baguette slices with butter, top with radishes, sprinkle with salt, and garnish with chives.

STACY'S PAIRING: A Sauvignon Blanc with a touch of tropical fruit flavor and mild acidity like Kontokosta Winery Sauvignon Blanc would nicely complement the creaminess and pungent pepperiness of this dish.

Mashed Potato Flatbread Topped with Poached Egg

FOR THE DOUGH

1½ pounds russet potatoes, peeled and quartered

2 teaspoons sugar

1½-ounce package active dry yeast

¼ cup olive oil

3 teaspoons sea salt

Freshly ground black pepper to taste

½ teaspoon ground cumin

2¼ cups all-purpose flour, plus more for rolling the dough

FOR THE TOPPING

2 medium Yukon Gold potatoes, peeled, cut into quarters

1 small red onion

1 bunch chives

2 garlic cloves

¼ cup olive oil, plus more for drizzling

½ teaspoon sea salt

6 ounces freshly grated Parmesan

¼ cup chopped fresh rosemary

Freshly ground black pepper to taste

My friend Jen makes a light-as-air, much anticipated potato bread that she serves every Easter. I wondered, if I added mashed potatoes to a flatbread mixture, would I get the same result? Pretty close.

This is a light, melt-in-your-mouth, flavorful flatbread made with potatoes two ways: mashed potatoes in the bread dough plus thinly sliced potatoes baked on top with rosemary and grated Parmesan.

It's my homage to the potato fields of the Hamptons. Wild potatoes were a staple food of the Sagaponack Native Americans, and later the Polish and Irish arrived to till the fields and build their fortunes with potatoes, which they easily found demand for in New York City. It's a foodstuff revered on Long Island as much for its unique heritage as for its versatility and flavor.

Crown this flatbread with a dressed arugula salad and a crocus-colored, farm fresh egg, barely poached, for a sophisticated appetizer or lunch. —*Hillary*

SERVES 4

1. Bring a pot of water to a boil, add the russet potatoes and cook until tender enough to mash, about 20 minutes. Drain and allow to cool for 10 minutes. Mash the potatoes with a fork or masher and then put them in the bowl of a stand mixer fitted with a dough hook.

2. Add the sugar to 1 cup warm water, stir, pour in the yeast, stir, and allow to rest for 8 minutes.

3. Pour the yeasty water over the mashed potatoes. Add the olive oil, salt, pepper, cumin, and flour; turn on the stand mixer and mix until smooth. Scoop the dough into a lightly oiled bowl, cover, place somewhere warm, and wait for about 1 hour, until it has doubled in size.

4. Meanwhile, preheat the oven to 450°F.

5. For the topping, slice the Yukon Gold potatoes paper thin and submerge them in a bowl of water to keep them from turning brown. Slice the red onion in half vertically, then slice each half horizontally into thin, half-moon slices. Thinly slice the chives.

6. Using a garlic press, press the garlic into the ¼ cup olive oil, add ½ teaspoon salt, and mix with a fork.

7. On a lightly floured work surface, roll out the dough to a large oval, or rectangle, and place it on a baking sheet lined with parchment paper and lightly brushed with olive oil. Brush the dough with the olive oil and garlic mixture.

8. Arrange the potato slices over the top. Sprinkle with the Parmesan, rosemary, onions, chives, and black pepper. Drizzle with a little olive oil and allow to rest for 20 minutes.

9. Make the dressing for the arugula salad by whisking the ¼ cup olive oil, lemon juice, and ½ teaspoon salt together. Toss over the arugula and mix to coat well.

10. Bake the flatbread 20 to 25 minutes, until golden brown.

11. While the flatbread is baking, poach 4 eggs by slipping them into about 3 inches of barely simmering water in a medium pan, cooking until just done to your liking, then removing them with a slotted spoon to a plate.

12. When you are ready to serve, slice the flatbread into individual portions, place on plates, cover each with the arugula mixture, and top with a poached egg.

STACY'S PAIRING: Any wine paired with this dish should have a touch of sweetness to match the richness of the egg, such as a rather dry Riesling or Gewürztraminer. Some Chardonnays could also work, like Paumanok Vineyards Festival Chardonnay with its crisp, yet fruity, character.

FOR THE SALAD
¼ cup extra virgin olive oil
½ lemon, juiced
½ teaspoon sea salt
4 cups baby arugula, washed
   and dried
4 large eggs, at room
   temperature

Asparagus Soup with Whipped Parmesan Cream

In the Hamptons, even the rain smells like the sea. My neighbor has a patch of asparagus, and in the spring, when it rains, I pull back the hedges to peek and see if his tender young shoots are pushing up yet. I live so close to the ocean that it could be that the rain brings with it special qualities, or at least I imagine it does. His asparagus love the salty rain. And I love receiving his gift of asparagus on my front porch.

Asparagus are the young spring shoots of a perennial flowering plant called sparrow grass. Fresh local shoots are so tender you can eat them raw with just a splash of good olive oil, a squeeze of lemon, with perhaps a shaving of Parmesan. If they are older, I make this soup with them.

Half the fun in making this soup is creating the savory whipped cream. All you need is a jar with a cover, heavy whipping cream, grated Parmesan, a hint of salt, and some enthusiastic shaking. When it has thickened, a generous dollop over a bowl of this woodsy-green soup delivers a delightful mouth surprise. —Hillary

SERVES 4

1. Cook the rice according to package instructions. Drain and reserve.

2. Wash and dry the asparagus. Slice each spear of the thick asparagus into 2-inch pieces. You don't have to bother to peel them. Slice the thin asparagus into ½-inch pieces and reserve.

3. Pour the olive oil into a medium frying pan and place over medium heat. Add the onion and garlic and cook until tender, about 3 minutes. Pour in the broth and bring to a boil. Slip the thicker pieces of asparagus into the boiling broth and cook until they are very soft. Take off the heat and cool the broth with the asparagus to room temperature.

4. Meanwhile, put the pieces of thin asparagus into a medium frying pan and cover with water. Bring to a boil and cook until just fork tender. Drain and reserve.

5. Working in two batches, put half the cooled broth with thick asparagus into a food processor or blender. Process for about 10 seconds, until smooth.

6. Pour the smooth asparagus mixture into a medium saucepan. Repeat this process for the second batch of broth with thick asparagus. Add 2 teaspoons sea salt and the black pepper.

7. Now you should have a pot of smooth asparagus soup. Add the cooked rice and cooked thin asparagus and stir to blend.

8. To make the savory whipped cream, pour the whipping cream into a jar, add the Parmesan and 1 teaspoon salt. Cover the jar and shake vigorously until the cream has thickened and can take shape. Or simply whip the cream with an electric mixer until soft peaks form, then whisk in the Parmesan and salt.

9. To serve the soup, heat it until hot. Divide it evenly between four bowls. Scoop a big dollop of the whipped cream onto the center of each bowl, dust the top of each dollop of cream with a little grated Parmesan, and serve.

½ cup basmati rice
1 pound thick asparagus, woody ends removed
1 pound thin asparagus, woody ends removed
2 tablespoons olive oil
½ medium white onion, minced
2 garlic cloves, minced
32 ounces chicken or vegetable stock (see page 230)
3 teaspoons sea salt
¼ teaspoon freshly ground black pepper
½ cup heavy whipping cream
3 tablespoons freshly grated Parmesan, plus more for garnish

STACY'S PAIRING: A crisp Pinot Grigio could work with all this flavorful greenness. Locally, I like the balancing effect that the bottom notes in Osprey's Dominion Gewürztraminer have on this springy dish.

Green Garlic Pesto Bites

**2 green garlic, bulbs and
leaves, or 5 scallions**

1 pound cream cheese

**1 cup coarse bread crumbs,
fresh or dried**

2 large eggs, lightly beaten

**1 tablespoon freshly grated
Parmigiano-Reggiano**

1 teaspoon sea salt

**½ teaspoon freshly grated
nutmeg**

**4 tablespoons (½ stick)
unsalted butter, melted**

Green garlic means spring. It arrives in April, before spinach and asparagus. Green garlic is the immature stage of any type of garlic, so it looks a lot like young leeks because its bulb has not yet divided into cloves. It tastes like the milder side of garlic. Its tender leaves remind me of the ramps I used to gather, as a child, from the foothills of the Allegheny Mountains.

In the next stage of garlic's development, each bulb sends up a "scape," or long stem, with a flower bud, from its center. Every year I plant more garlic in my garden than the year before—it's never enough.

I make these muffins small because they are so very rich. I like to use rye bread crumbs in these bites for added flavor. —*Stacy*

MAKES 4 DOZEN MINI MUFFINS

1. Preheat the oven to 375°F.

2. Trim the roots from below the garlic bulbs. (If a fleshy layer has started to form around the bulb, cut this layer off.) Soak the garlic in cool water for 10 minutes, then swish it around in the water to remove any soil. Rinse it and then spin dry. Use a very sharp knife to coarsely chop the garlic bulb and greens.

3. Place the garlic, cream cheese, bread crumbs, eggs, cheese, salt, and nutmeg in the bowl of a stand mixer. Run the mixer on medium and slowly pour the butter in while the mixer is running, mixing until well combined. You'll probably have to stop mixing to scrape the dough from the beater and the sides of the bowl once or twice.

4. Divide the dough among two mini muffin pans, lined with mini muffin papers, about 1 tablespoon per muffin cup.

5. Bake about 25 minutes, until the tops are golden brown. Serve warm or at room temperature.

STACY'S PAIRING: Seek out a white wine or a rosé that doesn't challenge the palate when combined with garlic and nutmeg. Locally, the soft, almost buttery Bridge Lane Rosé fits the bill.

JACKSON POLLOCK

These bites were inspired by the recipe for Spinach Muffins that appears in the book *Dinner with Jackson Pollock* by Robyn Lea. Lee Krasner and Jackson Pollock, in addition to being famous Abstract Expressionist painters, were well known in the Hamptons for their dinner parties.

The married couple moved from New York City to the hamlet of Springs in East Hampton in 1945. They bought a 19th-century farmhouse overlooking Accabonac Harbor in order to save money on living expenses and to enjoy the Hamptons golden light—the light that so many artists, such as Thomas Moran, William Merritt Chase, Larry Rivers, and Andy Warhol have been drawn to over the centuries.

Krasner and Pollock discovered their shared love of gathering food from local waters and from their own vegetable garden. Many an art critic, gallerist, and patron were beguiled around their dining table. The Pollock-Krasner House and Study Center, located in the artists' Springs residence, is open to the public from May through October. We recommend a visit to this historic studio and home. The house features the preserved mid-20th-century kitchen where Krasner and Pollock cooked. —*Stacy*

Spring Onion and Arugula Salad with Yogurt Dressing

FOR THE DRESSING

1½ cups plain yogurt

½ cup extra virgin olive oil

1 tablespoon pickled beet brine (optional)

2 teaspoons white wine vinegar

2 roasted garlic cloves (see opposite page)

1½ teaspoons sea salt

1 teaspoon ground cumin

½ teaspoon ground turmeric

¼ teaspoon freshly ground black pepper

⅛ teaspoon ground cayenne pepper

FOR THE SALAD

12 cups baby arugula

6 spring onions, chopped

¼ cup freshly snipped chives

Chive buds

Organic dandelion petals

We've included this salad for particular fans of spring onions and arugula, but we suggest offering it to a wider audience by using it as a hearty topping for fresh bread or a soup such as the Asparagus Soup with Whipped Parmesan Cream on page 28.

You can use scallions in place of the spring onions. Spring onions are similar in appearance to scallions, but have small bulbs at their base. They are planted in the fall for a spring harvest. The diminutive spring onion bulbs are sweeter and mellower than mature onions, but their greens are more intense in flavor than those of scallions.

Spring and early summer are the peak of dairy season, when domesticated ruminants such as goats, sheep, and cows have recently given birth. Use your favorite yogurt for this recipe—goat, sheep, or cow; whole fat, low-fat, or no fat. I make this dressing with Kalypso Greek Yogurt, a cow's milk yogurt that I purchase at my local farmers' market.

This dressing also makes a fine marinade for baked chicken. —Stacy

SERVES 6

1. Place all of the dressing ingredients in a food processor or blender and run on high until thoroughly combined, about 15 seconds. If you prefer a thinner dressing, beat in up to ¼ cup of water, 1 tablespoon at a time. Allow the dressing to rest for 10 minutes at room temperature.

2. Arrange the arugula in six salad bowls. Top with the onions and chives. Dollop the dressing on the salads. When ready to serve, garnish with some chive buds and dandelion petals.

STACY'S PAIRING: The acidity and floral aromas of a Gewürztraminer are a natural fit for the slight sweetness of the roasted garlic and yogurt. I also like Palmer Vineyards Albarino, with its hints of peach and green apple and its savory, lingering finish to go with this dish.

HOW TO ROAST AND CONFIT GARLIC

Both roasting and confiting garlic mellow its flavor and make it spreadable. —*Stacy*

Roasted Garlic

Whole head of garlic, unpeeled and unseparated
Olive oil
Sea salt to taste

1. Preheat the oven to 400°F.

2. Slice the upper clove tips off the head of garlic. Place the entire head in the center of a piece of heavy-duty aluminum foil. Drizzle the garlic with a bit of olive oil and salt. Cover the cut top of the head of garlic with a small piece of parchment paper. Seal the foil and place the package in a small baking dish.

3. Bake until the garlic is soft, about 45 minutes.

4. To use, separate cloves and squeeze them to release the roasted garlic paste.

5. Store the roasted garlic head in a sealed container in the refrigerator for up to a week, or in the freezer for up to 3 months.

Garlic Confit

Garlic cloves
Olive oil

The oil used to confit the garlic is very flavorful and may be used in combination with other oils in vinaigrettes, or as a finishing drizzle on fish or meat.

1. Preheat the oven to 200°F.

2. Place the garlic cloves in a small baking dish. Cover the cloves with olive oil. Bake the garlic until tender, about 90 minutes.

3. To store the garlic, allow it to cool and store it with enough oil to cover it in a sealed container in the refrigerator for up to 2 months.

Hamptons Bamboo Shoots and Roasted Vegetable Bowl

Serving this salad undressed preserves the flavors of the individual ingredients of the season: the slight nuttiness of the wheat berries (dried and hulled wheat kernels), the sweetness of the roasted root vegetables, and the grassy, artichoke-like flavor of the bamboo shoots. If you want to spice things up, prepare a vinaigrette of one part champagne vinegar and three parts fruity olive oil and use it on this salad. If you wish to tone down the garlic flavor, use roasted garlic (see page 33), instead of raw.

We've tried to give amounts that make it easy to shop for ingredients at your local farmers' market. But a "bunch" can vary widely, so if you're unsure about an amount, ask the farmer to weigh it for you. Most keep a scale at their stands.

I like to soak the wheat berries overnight, rather than just cooking them over prolonged high heat, as I find that the more intense method can render them a bit gluey. I serve this salad warm or at room temperature. It makes a great packed lunch. —*Stacy*

SERVES 6

1. Soak the wheat berries for about 8 hours in a nonreactive saucepan with at least 3 cups cold water. Add the kelp and bring to a boil, adding more water if needed. Boil for 30 minutes. Add the carrot and the ginger to the wheat berries and continue to boil until the wheat berries are softened but chewy, about 10 minutes more.

2. Meanwhile, preheat the oven to 400°F.

3. Place the parsnips, radishes, potatoes, and garlic in a large bowl. Pour the oil over the vegetables and toss to coat. Spread the vegetables out on a rimmed baking sheet lined with parchment paper. Bake for 20 minutes, then turn the vegetables over and bake until golden brown, about 20 minutes more.

4. Drain the wheat berries and stir in the bamboo shoots and salt to taste. Divide the wheat berry mixture among six serving bowls. Top with the roasted vegetables. Garnish with pieces of nori, if using, cilantro, and pansies just before serving.

Continued . . .

1 cup dried wheat berries

¼ cup Atlantic kelp or nori, broken into bite-size pieces

1 medium carrot, coarsely grated

2-inch piece ginger, peeled and grated

1 pound parsnips, thickly sliced

1 pound radishes, sliced

1 pound potatoes, thickly sliced

3 garlic cloves, crushed in a garlic press

¼ cup olive oil

6 fresh bamboo shoots (see page 36), blanched and coarsely chopped (or two 8-ounce cans bamboo shoots, rinsed and drained)

Kosher salt to taste

Nori (optional)

Cilantro leaves

Organic pansies

Healthy radish greens may be used in making the Radish Greens Pesto over a Tangle of Pasta on page 40.

Clean ginger peelings, including skin, may be used to make a tisane (a medicinal infusion).

STACY'S PAIRING: Locally, I like to pair this dish with Channing Daughters Winery Mudd Red Table Wine because both this wine and the fresh bamboo contain a hint of settled, salty iodine flavor. This red wine is a blend of Merlot, Syrah, Dornfelder, Cabernet Franc, and Blaufränkisch grapes. A light Grüner Veltliner would be a good alternative.

BAMBOO SHOOTS

Never plant bamboo. Bamboo is even more invasive than it is delicious. That being said, bamboo has long been a staple food in Asian countries, and bamboo shoots grow across many Hamptons lawns in the spring. Why not harvest them before they take over? I kick over shoots when they're about 8 inches tall and gather them up.

As with any wild food, take a sample to an expert in your area for identification before you even taste it. While the majority of bamboo varieties are edible to humans, some are not.

High in fiber, protein, copper, manganese, and zinc, fresh bamboo is far superior to the canned variety. But fresh shoots must be blanched.

TO BLANCH FRESH BAMBOO SHOOTS:

- Rinse in cold water to remove surface dirt.
- Use a very sharp, heavy knife or cleaver to cut about a half inch off the wider ends of the shoots.
- Carefully cut shoots in half lengthwise.
- Use the tips of your thumbs to separate the tender interior from the surrounding leaves and to pop the inside structure out.
- Place 1 teaspoon kosher salt in a medium saucepan. Fill the pan about three-quarters full of cold water and bring to a boil.
- Place all the shoots in the boiling water at once and cook for 7 minutes. Drain them and then shock them in a bowl of ice water for a few seconds. Drain them again to preserve their crunchiness. You may use the shoots when they have cooled to room temperature, or store them in the refrigerator for up to 1 week.

—Stacy

Butter Lettuce and Asparagus Salad with Warm Mustard Leaf Vinaigrette

This is a light spring salad; add cooked chicken, fish, or tofu for a heartier dish. Grade B New York State maple syrup has more flavor than Grade A. My mother and her family used to cook maple sap down. They sold the light, Grade A syrup and saved all of "the good dark stuff" for themselves. —*Stacy*

SERVES 4

1. Fill a deep bowl with ice water; set aside.

2. Break the woody ends off the asparagus spears.

3. Pour the wine and enough water into a large saucepan to total about an inch. Place a steamer basket in the pan, cover it, and bring the wine mixture to a boil. Add the asparagus to the basket and steam, covered, until crisp-tender, about 7 minutes. Shock the asparagus to stop the cooking by placing the spears in the bowl of ice water for a few seconds. Drain the asparagus and pat it dry. Cut the spears on the diagonal into bite-size pieces.

4. Divide and arrange the lettuce, radishes, and asparagus among four serving bowls.

5. To make the vinaigrette, stir the vinegar, oil, maple syrup, garlic, mustard seeds, the ½ teaspoon salt, and pepper together in a small saucepan. Gently stir in the mustard greens. Cover the pan and heat over very low heat until the greens are wilted, about 5 minutes.

6. Liberally spoon the vinaigrette over the salads. (I leave the mustard greens in the vinaigrette. You may prefer to remove them.) Garnish the salads with the pansy blossoms and serve immediately.

STACY'S PAIRING: If wine pairings were a game of cards, this sweet and sour dish featuring asparagus would be a joker. For tricky dishes such as this one, there is Riesling. With this salad, I like Raphael's semi-sweet Riesling with its notes of lime zest, apricots, and minerals, and its round, but acidic finish. Rieslings are also a godsend for pairing with spicy Chinese and Indian dishes.

FOR THE SALAD
1 bunch (about 1 pound) asparagus
½ cup white wine
8 ounces baby butter lettuce or other baby greens
20 small, colorful radishes, thinly sliced

FOR THE VINAIGRETTE
½ cup apple cider vinegar
½ cup olive oil
2 tablespoons maple syrup
1 garlic clove, crushed in a garlic press
1 tablespoon yellow mustard seeds
½ teaspoon fine sea salt
½ teaspoon freshly ground black pepper
1 cup baby mustard greens
Organic pansy blossoms

Healthy radish greens may be used in making the Radish Greens Pesto over a Tangle of Pasta on page 40.

Hamptons Fish Burger with Microgreens

1 tablespoon grapeseed oil

1¼ pounds raw white fish fillets (or 1 pound cooked fish)

Fine sea salt (to taste for raw fish)

Freshly ground black pepper, to taste for raw fish, or ½ teaspoon for cooked fish

1 medium carrot, grated

2 tablespoons freshly grated Parmigiano-Reggiano

2 tablespoons whole yellow mustard seeds

1 tablespoon chopped dried Atlantic kelp or nori (optional)

⅛ teaspoon ground white pepper

⅛ teaspoon smoked hot paprika

1 large egg, lightly beaten

Up to 1 cup Italian seasoned bread crumbs

Hot sauce (optional)

Burger buns (optional)

1 cup microgreens

Amagansett Sea Salt or other finishing salt

This recipe works well with a wide variety of fish, including salmon. You could use chopped clams, oysters, or cooked lobster, although they may become rather chewy in the oven. Some people like that. Hey, I like cheese in my fish—so no judgment here! —*Stacy*

MAKES 4 LARGE PATTIES

IF STARTING WITH RAW FISH:

1. Preheat the oven to 400°F. Line a baking sheet with parchment paper and brush with oil.

2. Place the fish fillets on the baking sheet, then turn them over to coat them in the oil. Sprinkle the fish with fine sea salt and pepper and place the sheet in the oven. Cook the fish about 10 minutes for each inch of thickness, just until it appears opaque. Remove the fish from the oven. Proceed to Step 1 below.

IF STARTING WITH COOKED FISH:

1. Preheat the oven to 350°F.

2. Place the cooked fish in a medium mixing bowl. Break up the fish with a fork and stir in the carrot, Parmigiano-Reggiano, mustard seeds, kelp, if using, ½ teaspoon black pepper, white pepper, and paprika. Then stir in the egg, followed by the bread crumbs. The amount of bread crumbs needed to create a firm consistency will vary with the types of fish used and the humidity. It may require up to a cup. Divide the burger mixture into four equal portions. Form each portion into a ball. Flatten the balls slightly to form patties.

3. Place the patties on the prepared baking sheet and bake for 10 minutes. Turn the patties over. Squirt the top of the patties with the hot sauce, if using. Bake about 5 minutes, until the patties are heated through.

4. Split the buns, if using, and place the patties on the buns, topping them with microgreens and finishing salt. Further dress and garnish the burger as you wish. Serve the patties hot.

STACY'S PAIRING: A light white wine or a light rosé works with this burger, as does a lightly caramel malt beer like Montauk Brewing Company Summer Ale.

MONTAUK FISH BURGER

In 2016, select Hamptons restaurants started serving the Montauk Fishburger in cooperation with Dock to Dish, a nonprofit organization focused on sustainable fishing. The recipe for the Montauk Fishburger was based on one created by Chef Eric Ripert of Le Bernardin, who is a fellow Hamptonite. The burger is decidedly fishy in flavor and is designed to make use of local fish that might otherwise go to waste. Hillary and I both enjoyed eating these burgers—we tried them together at the Almond Restaurant in Bridgehampton when they were first offered, and we recommend that you try them too. Our "Hamptons Fish Burger" is one that I have made at home for many years. It's not at all "fishy" tasting. It's based on a bean burger recipe that I made every week during my years as a vegetarian. —*Stacy*

Radish Greens Pesto over a Tangle of Pasta

4 cups tender radish greens, lightly packed

2 garlic cloves

¾ cup salted pumpkin seeds, plus ½ cup for garnish

½ lemon, juiced

½ teaspoon sea salt

⅛ teaspoon cayenne pepper

½ cup extra virgin olive oil

¼ cup grated Parmesan, plus more for garnish

Homemade Food Processor Pasta (recipe follows) or one 16-ounce package pasta

Great bunches of radishes come home with me from my forays to farms and their markets, spilling out of my well-worn gray-and-white-striped straw tote. It took me a while, but all of a sudden I realized what a shame it was to not use the large leafy radish greens.

When I read that they have as many antioxidants as kale or broccoli, and provide a serious punch of calcium and vitamin C, I decided to learn how to incorporate them into my cooking. What a delight to find that they have a surprisingly delicious earthy flavor.

One obvious way I thought to use them was to create a pesto-style recipe, which turned out to have a lovely vibrant green color and a great taste. I now use this pesto in a variety of ways, from topping crackers or tomato pizza to adding a spoonful as garnish for soup. I also sometimes mix it into hummus and serve it as a dip for vegetables.

Accompanying this recipe for the pesto, you will find my recipe for the homemade pasta I put it on. If you are pressed for time, substitute packaged pasta. —*Hillary*

SERVES 4

1. Fill a large bowl with water, drop the radish greens in, and swirl around vigorously to wash off any dirt. Drain the greens. Dry them on paper towels or in a salad spinner.

2. Put the radish greens, garlic, pumpkin seeds, lemon juice, salt, and cayenne into a food processor and pulse until finely chopped. With the machine running, drizzle in the olive oil until you have a smooth paste. Scoop the pesto into a bowl and stir in the cheese. Toss with cooked pasta (or follow recipe below for homemade pasta) and serve with additional pumpkin seeds and Parmesan as garnish.

STACY'S PAIRING: This dish cries out for an herbaceous Sauvignon Blanc, or for a light Chenin Blanc like Paumanok Vineyards Chenin Blanc Dry Table Wine.

1. Whisk the eggs, yolks, olive oil, and salt together, then pour into the bowl of a food processor.

2. Add the flour and process. If a ball forms, fine; stop there. If not, and you have fine pearls, that's okay too. Just scoop them out onto a piece of parchment paper and bring the dough together into a ball with your hands. Knead three or four times.

3. If the dough feels wet, add 1 tablespoon more of flour and knead it into the dough ball. Eggs vary in how liquid they are and in how much flour they can absorb, so start with the lesser amount, test with your finger, and add more if it seems sticky.

4. Wrap the dough ball in wax paper and allow it to rest for 30 to 45 minutes. Divide the dough ball into six pieces, working with one and covering the others.

5. Roll out, one by one, through a pasta machine. When you reach the #5 position, you may want to slice the sheet of dough in half if it has become too long. I roll my pasta to the #8 position, or very thinly, before feeding it through the cutters.

6. If you are working by hand, roll out the dough as thinly as you can with a rolling pin, then cut the dough into pasta with a sharp knife or pizza cutter. Either way, use no extra flour, or as little as possible, since adding flour will make the pasta a bit gooey when cooked.

7. Hang the pasta as you cut it on the backs of chairs covered with clean towels.

8. When it is all done, drop into boiling water to cook. Depending on how thinly you rolled your dough and what width of pasta you cut, it could take from 30 seconds to 2 minutes to cook, so stand nearby and test a strand to see when it gets to a good place for you.

9. Drain, toss with the pesto, divide between four plates, then garnish with pumpkin seeds and grated cheese.

Homemade Food Processor Pasta

SERVES 4

2 large eggs, at room temperature
4 large egg yolks, at room temperature
2 teaspoons extra virgin olive oil
¼ teaspoon fine sea salt
2 cups flour, plus more if needed

The egg whites may be refrigerated in a sealed container for up to 4 days for another use.

Poached Cod and Clams in Buttered Broth

FOR THE DRIZZLE

½ cup extra virgin olive oil

½ teaspoon Dijon mustard

1 organic lemon, zested and juiced

1 small shallot, minced

3 tablespoons minced fresh basil

1 tablespoon minced fresh flat-leaf parsley

2 teaspoons small capers

2 garlic cloves, minced

½ teaspoon sea salt

Clamming in the Hamptons is a local tradition and a fun way to get the clams for this dish. You can go to a local town hall and buy an inexpensive clamming permit, along with a map showing you where to forage your own fresh clams. Go at low tide with a bucket and a rake or a big spoon to dig for them. You can tell where clams are by looking for air bubbles in the wet sand. Keep clams in damp sand in your bucket until you get home, and use them the same day.

Otherwise, to make this recipe, buy the clams, as well as really fresh cod, at a good fish market. Pick up clam juice or fish stock while you are there.

This dish becomes electrified with flavor when drizzled with virgin sauce, which pulls all the elements together. The origin is the French sauce called *vierge,* meaning virgin, which means the ingredients are raw. —*Hillary*

SERVES 4

1. To make the drizzle, put the olive oil into a medium bowl with the mustard and whisk to combine. Add the rest of the sauce ingredients and stir to combine. Reserve at room temperature.

2. To make the fish and clams, rinse the clams under cold running water and scrub them to remove any outside sand or grit. Discard any clams that are not tightly closed (these are already dead and thus inedible).

3. Cook the noodles according to package instructions and toss them with 2 tablespoons of the olive oil until well coated. Cover to keep them warm.

4. Meanwhile, rinse and drain the parsley. Remove the leaves and mince them. Reserve.

5. Pour 3 tablespoons of the olive oil into a large saucepan and warm over medium heat. Add the garlic and onion and cook until tender, about 4 minutes. Pour in the clam broth and stir in the salt. This will be your poaching liquid.

6. Bring the broth to a boil, reduce to a gentle simmer, add the clams, cover and cook until they open. The time required will depend on the size of the clams. Remove to a plate with a slotted spoon as they open. Tent the plate with aluminum foil.

7. Lower the cod fillets into the broth, cover, and gently simmer until just cooked (opaque and slightly firm to the touch), about 5 to 6 minutes. Remove to a plate and tent with aluminum foil.

8. Turn up the heat on the broth, bring to a boil, then reduce to a vigorous simmer and cook for 3 minutes to reduce the sauce and concentrate the flavor. Add a few drops of fresh lemon juice and stir. Add the butter and whisk until melted. Taste and add salt and pepper if desired.

9. To serve, arrange the cooked noodles in each bowl, place a fillet of cod on the top, and surround it with four clams. Divide all of the hot broth evenly over the top of each fillet. Drizzle with the virgin sauce. Generously garnish each bowl with minced parsley, quartered lemons, and serve with a small bowl of sea salt flakes and slices of baguette to sop up any remaining broth.

STACY'S PAIRING: A zippy wine like Lieb Cellars Reserve Pinot Blanc serves this buttery dish well. Its hints of lemon and lime zest complement the fish.

FOR THE POACHED COD AND CLAMS

16 little neck or cherrystone clams
One 16-ounce package egg noodles
3 tablespoons olive oil
½ bunch flat-leaf parsley
4 garlic cloves, minced
1 medium white onion, minced
24 ounces clam broth or fish stock
1 teaspoon sea salt
Four 4-ounce cod fillets, skinless
Few drops lemon juice
2 tablespoons unsalted butter
Good olive oil for garnish
2 lemons, quartered for garnish
Sea salt flakes for serving
Sliced baguette for serving

CLAMS

TYPES OF CLAMS

Quahogs: really large, hard-shell clams that are typically used for making clam chowder.

Cherrystone: medium quahogs, which are great for grilling, pasta dishes, or stuffed.

Little Neck: small with deep shells. Little Necks are sweet and are often served raw on the half shell.

Steamers: oblong soft-shell clams with brittle thin shells that can break easily. They have a neck protruding from one end. These are the "steamers" that are often served with melted butter for you to dunk them in.

HOW TO BUY THEM

Clams should be alive when you buy them. You can test them. They should be slightly open, and when you tap on their shells, they should snap shut. If they don't close, throw them away. If there are any that have broken shells, throw them away.

If they are packed in a plastic bag at the store, ask the fishmonger to keep the top of the bag open so the clams can breathe.

Bring them home and place them in a colander over a plate in the refrigerator until you are ready to use them, preferably the same day.

Use a brush to scrub the shells of the clams under cold running water.

HOW TO COOK THEM

Add water or wine to a pan, bring it to a boil, add the clams, cover, and steam until they open. The time required will depend on the size of the clams. Throw away any that do not open. —Hillary

Spring Spatchcocked Chicken Pan Supper

4-pound whole organic chicken

2 small branches fresh rosemary or sage leaves

2 medium potatoes (about 1 pound), coarsely chopped

3 medium parsnips (about 12 ounces), coarsely chopped

12 small sunchokes or radishes (about 8 ounces)

1 small bunch (about 4 ounces) green onions or pencil-size leeks or ramps, whites and greens, coarsely chopped

⅓ cup olive oil

4 tablespoons (½ stick) unsalted butter, melted

1 tablespoon dried chives

1 teaspoon freshly ground black pepper, plus more for sprinkling

½ teaspoon ground white pepper

1 teaspoon kosher salt, plus more for sprinkling

Fresh chives

This is a hearty back-to-basics meal that gives natural flavors depth by concentrating them—tubers, roots, peppers, chives, and fats meld and complement one another. Feel free to change up the mix of root vegetables by using carrots or turnips to total the same amount. Just be sure to cut them all to about the same size so that they cook evenly.

When I cook this dish for just my husband and me, I cut down only one side of the chicken's backbone to spatchcock it, leaving the backbone to roast along with the rest of the bird. This way, the backbone is already roasted for my future stock-making. —*Stacy*

SERVES 4

1. Preheat the oven to 400°F.

2. To spatchcock the chicken, use kitchen shears to cut along each side of the backbone and remove it for another use. Splay the bird out, cut side down in the center of a half-size baking sheet (13 by 18 inches), and push on its breast with your hands to flatten it out somewhat. Trim off the wing tips and reserve them for use in making stock. Use a sharp knife to make a puncture from the neck end of the bird about 2 inches into the thickest part of each breast. Use your fingers to insert a rosemary branch deeply into each of these pockets.

3. Place the potatoes, parsnips, sunchokes, and green onions in a large bowl and drizzle them with the oil and melted butter. Sprinkle the vegetables with the dried chives, both peppers, and salt. Stir to coat. Use a slotted spoon to move all of the vegetables to the baking sheet, spreading them out around the bird. Use your hands to rub the leftover liquid from the bowl over the entire surface (top and bottom) of the chicken. Sprinkle the bird with additional salt and ground black pepper.

4. Bake the chicken for about 1 hour, until it is golden brown and registers 165°F with an instant-read thermometer in the thickest part of the thigh. Remove the bird from the oven to a platter to rest.

5. Reduce the oven temperature to 300°F. Turn the vegetables over and stir them around on the baking sheet. Put the pan back into the oven to stay hot while the bird rests for 15 minutes. Garnish with fresh chives and serve the chicken and vegetables immediately.

STACY'S PAIRING: The fruity acidity of a Trebbiano grape wine like Wölffer Estate Vineyard Trebbiano complements the richness of this dish nicely. Alternatively, a dark English porter style beer with notes of coffee like Greenport Harbor Brewing Company Black Duck Porter provides a nice contrast to the light flavors at work in this meal.

Flounder Swimming in Merlot

2 pounds white fish fillets, such as winter flounder, fluke (a.k.a. summer flounder), or cod

Grapeseed oil or olive oil

½ teaspoon kosher salt, plus more to taste

Freshly ground black pepper to taste

1 cup Merlot

2 tablespoons red wine vinegar

2 garlic cloves, unpeeled and smashed

1 teaspoon ground cumin

¼ teaspoon ground cayenne pepper

6 Dried Squash Blossoms (recipe follows) or ¼ teaspoon saffron

2 teaspoons unsalted butter

24 cups (about 15 ounces) baby spinach

Sag Harbor Village is my family's chosen hometown. We love its walkability, its rich history, and its friendly local population. In the early 19th century, the old whaling port of Sag Harbor was a layover for sailors from all over the world. A number of Portuguese sailors adopted Sag Harbor as their home. Though Long Island's East End never had a Portuguese enclave such as those in New Bedford, Massachusetts, and Providence, Rhode Island, Portuguese cuisine nonetheless continues to exert a delicious influence here on Long Island.

This baked fish dish was inspired by *vinho d'alhos,* a traditional Portuguese dish typically prepared atop a stove or grill. *Vinho* means wine, *alhos* is garlic. I've included instructions for baking or grilling this dish. If you have ceramic rarebits, they work really well for serving this fish.

If you happen to have the remains of a bottle of Merlot that has just begun to turn to vinegar, you can use that for both the wine and the vinegar in this recipe. (We've had only a bottle of Merlot start to turn to vinegar once at our house—that bottle was a jeroboam!)

The dried squash blossoms in this dish came about because I had a dozen fresh blossoms in my refrigerator on a July day awaiting stuffing for dinner that evening, but then a sudden invitation to dine out came up. I decided to try drying the blossoms in the oven to preserve them. What a discovery! I've taken to using them in dishes that call for saffron. Though there is no equivalent for saffron, the pollen and petals of these dried blossoms do provide a nice, full undernote of flavor to dishes. I keep a jarful in my freezer all year now. —*Stacy*

SERVES 4

TO BAKE THE FISH:

1. Allow refrigerated fish to rest at room temperature for about 30 minutes.

2. Preheat the oven to 400°F.

3. Line a baking sheet with parchment paper and brush with oil. Lay the fish fillets on the prepared baking sheet. Turn the fillets over to coat them. Sprinkle with salt and pepper. Bake about 10 minutes per inch of thickness, until the fish flakes easily.

4. Meanwhile, stir the Merlot, vinegar, garlic, cumin, ½ teaspoon salt, cayenne, and blossoms together in a very large frying pan. Simmer over low heat for about 5 minutes. Remove the garlic and squash blossoms. Add the butter and stir it in until melted.

5. Add the spinach to the frying pan and stir to coat. Cover the spinach for a couple minutes to wilt it. Leave the frying pan on the burner over lowest heat until ready to serve.

6. Remove the fish from the oven and drain it.

7. Make beds of prepared spinach on the serving plates for the fish and place the fillets atop the spinach. Use a teaspoon to drizzle extra sauce from the pan of spinach over the fish. Serve immediately.

Continued . . .

TO GRILL THE FISH:

1. Allow refrigerated fish to come to room temperature for about 30 minutes.

2. Set up the grill for direct grilling and preheat to high.

3. Make individual "boats" of heavy-duty aluminum foil a little larger than the fish fillets to hold them on the grill by folding a doubled sheet of foil inward. Coat the inside bottoms of the boats with oil and place the fillets in them. Sprinkle with salt and pepper. Place the boats on the grill for about 7 minutes, until the fish flakes easily with a fork. (Thicker fillets will have to be turned over after a few minutes. Follow steps 4 through 7.

Dried Squash Blossoms

MAKES 12 BLOSSOMS

1 dozen squash blossoms

1. Preheat the oven to 200°F.

2. Gently wipe blossoms clean with a soft brush. Cut each blossom in half through its base. Lay the blossom halves on a baking sheet lined with parchment paper, cut side up. Bake for 30 minutes. Turn the oven off and leave the blossoms in the closed oven until fully dry, about 30 minutes more. If you intend to freeze them, allow the blossoms to cool for 5 minutes outside of the oven before packaging.

STACY'S PAIRING: It may seem like Merlot would be the perfect wine to pair with a dish containing Merlot, but the vinegar in this dish so transforms the character of the wine that a better pairing would be a glass (or, indeed, several glasses) of a medium-bodied Cabernet Franc. But locally, I like to pair it with Channing Daughters Winery Mosaico, a uniquely savory white blend of Pinot Grigio, Chardonnay, Sauvignon Blanc, Muscat Ottonel, Gewürztraminer, and Friulano, aged in oak.

Strawberry Layer Cake with Rhubarb Jam Filling

8 tablespoons (1 stick) unsalted butter, at room temperature, plus additional butter for the pans

2¼ cups cake flour, plus additional flour for the pans

1 pound fresh strawberries, hulled and pureed to make 1½ cups

1¼ cups sugar

2 large eggs

2½ teaspoons double-acting baking powder

1 teaspoon pure vanilla extract

½ teaspoon baking soda

½ teaspoon kosher salt

1 cup rhubarb jam (the recipe that follows makes 5 cups)

1 batch Buttermilk-Cream Cheese Frosting (recipe follows)

1 pint fresh strawberries for garnish

Many people have a fond recollection of a grandmother who used to make them strawberry-rhubarb pie. But did they really love the dish? I like the flavor combination, but to me the texture of that pie has always left a lot to be desired. (Sorry, Gram.) So, I made it into a cake—loads of flavor, and nothing but pleasant textures. Gram always told me that cake ingredients blend together much more easily if they are at the same temperature. So, allow the berries and the eggs to come to room temperature if they have been refrigerated.

Rhubarb is one of the rare jams for which I recommend the use of liquid pectin, rather than powdered Pomona's Universal Pectin, in order to achieve the desired flavor and texture. Not all rhubarb stalks turn red when they're ready for harvest. Green stalks work fine—but you might want to replace one-quarter cup of their juice with red raspberry juice in this recipe to add color to the jam.

I prefer freezing fresh rhubarb from my garden, rather than stewing it to break it down for jam making, because freezing preserves its flavor and color.

I like to use frosting on top and as a filling. This frosting recipe makes enough to thoroughly frost this cake in the traditional manner, so you may choose to halve it. —*Stacy*

SERVES 12

1. Preheat the oven to 375°F. Grease and flour the bottoms and sides of two 8-inch layer cake pans. Line the pan bottoms with parchment paper cut to fit. Grease and flour the top of the paper.

2. Place the pureed berries, butter, cake flour, sugar, eggs, baking powder, vanilla, baking soda, and kosher salt in the bowl of a stand mixer. Beat the batter at low speed until well mixed, scraping the beater and the sides of bowl as needed. Then beat at high speed for 5 minutes, occasionally scraping down the sides of the bowl.

3. Divide the batter evenly between the prepared pans and bake about 25 minutes, until the cake layers are golden brown and springy. Cool the cake layers in the pans on a wire rack for 10 minutes, then carefully remove each cake layer from its pan by running a plastic knife around its outer edges and gently inverting the cake layers onto a wire rack to cool to room temperature.

Continued . . .

Homemade Rhubarb Jam Filling

MAKES 5 CUPS

3 cups frozen rhubarb
  (2 pounds) and its juice,
  thawed
5½ cups sugar
One 3-ounce pouch liquid
  pectin

Buttermilk–Cream Cheese Frosting

MAKES 3 CUPS

One 16-ounce package
  confectioners' sugar
3 tablespoons unsalted butter, at room temperature
3 tablespoons cream cheese,
  at room temperature
3 tablespoons whole milk,
  more if necessary
1 tablespoon white balsamic
  vinegar
1½ teaspoons pure vanilla
  extract
⅛ teaspoon fine sea salt

1. Place the rhubarb (and its juice) and the sugar in a large pot and stir to combine. The pot must not be more than one-third full in order to allow room for a full, rolling boil (a boil that cannot be stirred down). Bring the fruit mixture to a full, rolling boil over high heat. Stir in the pectin and boil hard for 1 minute, stirring constantly. Remove the pot from the heat.

2. Allow 1 cup of jam to cool fully for use on the cake. If you wish, can some of the jam in jars; follow standard water bath canning directions.

1. Combine all the frosting ingredients in the bowl of a stand mixer. Blend until very smooth, adding more milk, if necessary, 1 teaspoon at a time, to make the frosting a good spreading consistency.

2. To assemble the cake, place one of the cake layers onto a cake plate. Spread jam over the top of this bottom cake layer, avoiding the edges. Place the second cake layer, centered, over the bottom layer. Frost the cake and, just before serving, garnish with the fresh berries or flowers.

STACY'S PAIRING: The complexity and sweetness of this dish calls for a very simple dessert wine, such as Duck Walk Vineyards "one-note wonder," Aphrodite, a late harvest Gewürztraminer.

Fresh Mint Ice Cream with Chocolate Sauce

The mint ice cream served at ice cream stores usually has a neon green color and bears no resemblance to this ice cream, which is made with fresh mint leaves and has a natural botanical color and really minty flavor.

If you would like a more traditional mint ice cream color, try adding 2 tablespoons of crème de menthe to the ice cream mixture, but please, oh please, don't add green food coloring or mint extract. Trust me on this one.

Drizzle a swirl of the warm chocolate sauce over the ice cream, or go crazy and melt down some Thin Mints to lavishly drape your scoop. —*Hillary*

MAKES 1 QUART

1. Wash and dry the mint leaves.

2. Pour the milk into a small saucepan and bring it just to the point where it looks like it will start to boil. Take it off the heat, roughly tear the mint leaves and add them into the milk, cover, and allow to infuse for 30 minutes.

3. In the meantime, in another small saucepan, whisk 1 cup of the cream with the cornstarch until it is dissolved. Then heat the mixture over medium-low heat and cook, whisking frequently, until slightly thickened, for 3 to 4 minutes. Add the sugar and whisk until dissolved. Pour the cream mixture into a food processor. Add the infused mint milk, the remaining cup of cream, and vanilla, and then process until the mint is finely chopped.

4. Pour the mixture into a container and put it in the refrigerator for 4 hours.

5. Process the mixture in an ice cream maker for about 25 minutes. Line a small loaf pan with plastic wrap, leaving a couple of inches hanging over each end. Scoop the ice cream into the pan and freeze for at least 4 hours, until firm.

6. To make the chocolate sauce, heat the 1 cup cream, 1 teaspoon vanilla, and butter in a small saucepan over medium heat. Add the chocolate and stir until totally melted. Keep the sauce warm.

7. Remove the ice cream from the freezer. Unmold it onto a plate and remove the plastic wrap. Dip a sharp knife in hot water and use it to slice the ice cream. Place one slice on each plate, drizzle decoratively with the chocolate sauce, and serve.

FOR THE ICE CREAM
2½ cups fresh mint leaves, tightly packed
1 cup whole milk
2 cups heavy cream
1 tablespoon cornstarch
¾ cup sugar
1 teaspoon pure vanilla extract

FOR THE CHOCOLATE SAUCE
1 cup heavy cream
1 teaspoon pure vanilla extract
2 tablespoons unsalted butter
8 ounces semi-sweet chocolate, coarsely chopped

Clean mint trimmings can be used to make a tisane.

STACY'S PAIRING: How about a nice hot cup of herbal mint tea?

Sweet Carrot Flan

1¾ cups heavy whipping
   cream
1 cup whole milk
⅛ teaspoon kosher salt
1½ cups sugar
1 medium carrot, peeled and
   shredded into ribbons
3 large eggs
2 large egg yolks
½ teaspoon hazelnut or
   almond extract

Hillary wanted to try using carrots in a dessert other than cake. We considered making flan or pudding or macaroons. It was going to be her recipe to develop, but I got to feeling a little abashed because it had been so long since I'd made a flan. So, I whipped one up and dappled it with carrot.

This flan can be made up to two days ahead. —*Stacy*

SERVES 8

1. Combine the cream, milk, and salt in a medium saucepan. Bring to a simmer over medium heat. Turn the heat off and allow the mixture to rest for about 30 minutes.

2. Preheat the oven to 350°F.

3. To make the caramel, combine the sugar and ⅓ cup water in a small, heavy frying pan. Stir over low heat until the sugar dissolves. Increase the heat to medium-high and cook, stirring, until the syrup turns amber, about 12 minutes. Quickly pour the syrup into a 9-inch glass pie plate. Rotate the pie plate to coat its sides.

4. Arrange the carrot evenly over the bottom of the pie plate.

5. Whisk the eggs, egg yolks, hazelnut extract, and the remaining ½ cup sugar in a stand mixer just until blended. Gradually beat the cream mixture into the egg mixture until well incorporated, not more than 1 minute. Pour the custard through a sieve into the pie plate.

6. Pour ½ inch of hot water into the large cast-iron frying pan. Place the pie plate in the frying pan water bath. Bake about 40 minutes, until the flan is gently set. Transfer the flan to a rack to cool, then refrigerate it until cold, about 2 hours. Cover the flan and keep it in the refrigerator until you're ready to serve it.

7. To serve, run a plastic knife around the sides of the flan to loosen it. Cover the flan with a serving plate and turn the flan over onto the plate. Carefully lift off the pie plate, allowing the caramel syrup to run over the flan.

The egg whites may be refrigerated in a sealed container for up to 4 days for another use.

STACY'S PAIRING: A very sweet white wine like a Riesling suits this delicate dessert. Pindar Vineyards Winter White, with its floral aromas, does not overpower this dish. It's a blend of Chardonnay, Sauvignon Blanc, Riesling, and Cayuga grapes.

Potato Cheesecake with Caramel Crust

FOR THE CRUST

3 tablespoons unsalted butter, melted, plus more for pan

Flour for the pan

1¼ cups graham cracker crumbs (approximately 9 crackers)

3 tablespoons sugar

FOR THE FILLING

1 pound cream cheese, at room temperature

15 ounces ricotta

1 cup sour cream

1 cup sugar

1 tablespoon pure vanilla extract

¼ teaspoon nutmeg, freshly grated

4 eggs, lightly beaten

1 large boiling potato (about 10 ounces), cooked, peeled, and grated

FOR THE CARAMEL LAYER (OPTIONAL)

4 tablespoons (½ stick) unsalted butter

½ cup sugar

½ teaspoon kosher salt

This dish was inspired by a cooking demonstration put on by Colonial food historian Diane Fish at Bay Street Theater in Sag Harbor. She explained that before globalization as we know it, housewives made spring desserts from what they had on hand—the last potatoes in the cellar and fresh dairy products. And it was good.

The potato and ricotta give this cheesecake an interesting texture. If you'd prefer a smoother cheesecake, you can run the potato and cheese mixture through a food processor, after it has been mixed. Just don't be tempted to skip the step of grating the cooked potato first—otherwise, the filling could be gluey.

Caramel loves to stick, so use a very thin metal spatula to free the crust from the pan bottom. When storing leftover cheesecake, remove it to another pan before refrigerating. —*Stacy*

SERVES 8

1. Preheat the oven to 325°F. Butter and flour the bottom and sides of a 10-inch springform pan.

2. In a medium mixing bowl, mix the graham cracker crumbs, 3 tablespoons butter, and 3 tablespoons sugar together. Press firmly onto the bottom of the springform pan. Bake the crust for about 15 minutes, until lightly browned. Remove the crust from the oven, leaving the oven on.

3. For the filling, place the cream cheese, ricotta, sour cream, 1 cup sugar, vanilla extract, and nutmeg together in the bowl of a stand mixer. Mix until well blended. Mix in the eggs. Mix in the potato just until incorporated.

4. To make the caramel layer (if using), combine the ¼ cup butter, ½ cup sugar, and salt in a small saucepan. Bring to a boil over medium heat and let bubble, whisking occasionally, until light golden brown, about 5 minutes. Pour the caramel over the crust using a circular motion to form a large round shape. Avoid pouring any caramel onto the crust within about an inch of the sides of the pan.

5. Pour the cheese filling over the caramel and crust. Bake about 1 hour 15 minutes, until the center is almost set. Turn the oven off and leave the cheesecake in the closed oven for at least 1 hour to cool and firm up. Take the cheesecake out of the oven, allow it to come to room temperature, then chill it in the refrigerator before serving.

STACY'S PAIRING: Potato vodka—like Sagaponacka Potato Vodka, with its strong vanilla notes—is a natural fit.

Traditional Strawberry Shortcake

Climates change but strawberry shortcake remains a universal favorite.

When I moved to the Hamptons 20 years ago, it was risky to schedule a strawberry social in mid-June. Now local strawberries start to trickle into the South Fork farm stands right around Memorial Day.

In 2004, I volunteered to help prepare the main attraction at a strawberry social. I was shocked that the cook in charge used Bisquick mix to make the short cakes. In the place and time I'm from (North Otto, New York, in the 1980s), scratch cooking was part of the social contract. For instance, my mom's potato salad and Mrs. Bird's (our old neighbor) blueberry pie and the Otto Fire Department's barbeque chicken contained no convenience foods.

I suggest adding a cooked egg yolk to the biscuit for a touch more richness, if that appeals.

Substitute any soft summer fruit for the strawberries, such as raspberries, blueberries, or chopped peaches, adjusting sugar to taste. Blueberries need to be crushed slightly to prevent them from rolling off the cake. I cut the biscuit dough into four, or eight, rectangles for serving. I know my audience.

To get the most lift in your whipped cream, make sure that the mixing bowl and beaters are perfectly dry and chilled before you whip the cream. —Stacy

SERVES 4 TO 8

1. Dust the bottom of a loaf pan with flour.

2. To make the shortcake biscuits, place the flour, 3 tablespoons of the sugar, baking powder, and salt in the work bowl of a food processor. (Cover any openings so that you don't get dusted with ingredients.) Pulse to combine. Running the processor on low, add the butter a piece at a time and mix until the dough resembles coarse crumbs. Mix in the hard-boiled egg yolk, if using. Continue to mix on low while slowly pouring in the cream, mixing just until the dough comes together. Turn the dough into the loaf pan and gently pat it flat. Cover and refrigerate the dough for 1 hour.

3. Line a baking sheet with parchment paper and sprinkle it generously with the cornmeal, if using. Preheat the oven to 375°F.

Continued . . .

1⅔ cups all-purpose flour, additional flour to dust the loaf pan

⅓ cup plus 3 tablespoons sugar

1 tablespoon baking powder

⅛ teaspoon kosher salt

6 tablespoons very cold, unsalted butter, cut into 6 pieces, plus additional for buttering the biscuits

1 hard-boiled egg yolk (optional)

⅔ cup cold heavy whipping cream or whole buttermilk

2 teaspoons fine cornmeal (optional)

1 quart fresh strawberries, hulled and sliced, reserving 8 whole berries for garnish

1 tablespoon white wine vinegar

1 cup heavy whipping cream, well chilled

Fresh mint for garnish

4. Run a knife around the edge of the dough. Invert the loaf pan onto the prepared baking sheet to release the dough. Cut the dough into four to eight biscuits. If biscuits break apart at all, just recombine them with your hands. Position the biscuits at least 1 inch apart on the prepared baking sheet. Bake 20 to 25 minutes, until the biscuits are golden brown. Transfer them to a wire rack to cool.

5. To prepare the fruit, in a medium mixing bowl, add the sliced strawberries and gently stir in the remaining $\frac{1}{3}$ cup sugar and the vinegar into the sliced berries. Cover and allow the fruit to macerate at room temperature for about 30 minutes.

6. To prepare the topping, whip the cream in a stand mixer just until it forms stiff peaks.

7. To serve, slice the biscuits in half horizontally and butter the cut sides of the biscuits. Drain the berries, reserving their syrup. Cover a biscuit half with berries, layer on the other biscuit half, cover that with berries and top with a dollop of whipped cream. Drizzle with the leftover syrup and garnish with mint and reserved berries. Serve immediately.

STACY'S PAIRING: Serving this dish for breakfast with tea is a family favorite at my house. When they hear the stand mixer whipping the cream, everyone is suddenly wide awake and ready to face the day.

Chapter Two

LOW SUMMER

Memorial Day to the Fourth of July

Warm evenings encourage walks through vineyards full of growing vines reaching for the Hamptons sun, excursions to farmers' markets and roadside farm stands, fishing off Montauk, and dining alfresco with friends by candlelight. The recipes in this chapter celebrate the harvest of early summer.

SMALL PLATES

Baked Stuffed Zucchini Blossoms 66

Kale Chips 68

Kale Poppers 70

Mile-High Crustless Vegetable Pie 72

SALADS

Strawberry and Spinach Salad with Chopped Feta Vinaigrette 74

Summer Solstice Salad 76

Beet-Stained Potato Salad with Chunky Scallions 78

Umami Bomb Bread Salad 79

MAINS

Hamptons Famous Fresh Clam Pie 80

Broiled Bluefish with Parmesan Panko Crust 83

Blue Cheese Chicken with Strawberry Salsa 84

Long Island Duck Breasts with Duck Walk Vineyards Blueberry Port Sauce 86

Steak Picnic Sandwiches with Whole Cherry Tomato Jam 88

DESSERTS

Strawberry Sour Cream Ice Cream 90

Cherry Sweet Cheese Pocket Pies 92

Red Berry Pudding in Mason Jars 94

Swiss Chard and Sag Harbor Rum Pie with Rum Custard Sauce 96

Baked Stuffed Zucchini Blossoms

8 zucchini blossoms
1 cup whole milk ricotta
¼ cup finely grated Pecorino Romano
3 eggs
¼ teaspoon sea salt
¾ cup Italian seasoned bread crumbs

Buttery gold to deep shades of orange, delicate zucchini blossoms, also referred to as squash blossoms, can be found in markets from spring through late summer. I've even found them growing wild by the side of the road where I take my morning walk, colonizing an unlikely patch of earth and thriving near the sea. The wildflowers I pick go into vases, the squash blossoms into the oven.

To keep it light, rather than the more traditional method of frying the blossoms, I stuff them with a fluffy ricotta cheese mixture and bake them. They arrive hot, soft on the inside and crispy on the outside, making a superb appetizer. If you like, you can set them on a pool of tomato sauce for added color and interest. —Hillary

SERVES 4

1. Preheat the oven to 400°F.

2. Using tweezers, or small scissors, carefully remove the stamen from the inside of each blossom. If the blossoms are dusty, rinse them gently and pat dry.

3. In a medium-size mixing bowl, stir together the ricotta, Pecorino Romano, 1 beaten egg, and salt.

4. Place 2 lightly beaten eggs in a shallow bowl. Pour the bread crumbs onto a dinner plate.

5. Carefully spoon the cheese mixture into each blossom and twist the ends slightly to seal. Gently drag the blossoms through the beaten eggs to thoroughly coat them. Then roll the blossoms in the bread crumbs to lightly coat. Place the blossoms on a baking sheet line with parchment paper.

6. Bake about 10 minutes, until golden and crispy on the outside. Remove from the oven and serve hot, two on each plate.

STACY'S PAIRING: The creaminess of this dish demands some acidity. Channing Daughters Winery Rosato di Sculpture Garden fits the bill with its pronounced tartness. It's a field blend of Merlot, Blaufränkisch, and Teroldego grapes. A full-bodied Chardonnay could also work well.

Kale Chips

1 small bunch (about
   8 ounces) fresh kale, stems
   and large spines removed
1½ teaspoons apple cider
   vinegar
1 tablespoon olive oil
½ teaspoon fine sea salt
Pink peppercorns, crushed
   (optional)

Customers at the Sag Harbor Farmers Market often ask me how to make kale chips. It's super simple. The basic recipe for kale chips, which I've tweaked, was handed down to me from a true kale authority. Bette Lacina of Bette & Dale's Organic Farm in Sag Harbor was growing kale and eating leafy greens three times a day years before any of her customers had ever made a green smoothie. And her last name is almost the same as the name of lacinato kale, or cavolo nero ("black cabbage") kale. Lacinato is a good choice for both the kale poppers and chips recipes, but even the really curly stuff will work just fine.

Collard greens, cabbage leaves, and even young horseradish leaves can be used instead of the kale. Just keep a close eye on the chips while they bake to avoid burning them. —Stacy

SERVES 4

1. Preheat the oven to 350˚F.

2. Rinse the kale, pat it dry, and place it in a large mixing bowl. Drizzle the kale with the vinegar. Toss the leaves with your hands to coat them. Drizzle the kale with the olive oil and again toss the leaves with your hands to coat the leaves.

3. Spread the kale in a single layer over the three baking sheets lined with parchment paper. Sprinkle the salt evenly over the leaves.

4. Bake the chips for about 12 minutes, until they're crispy. Sprinkle with pepper, if using. Serve warm or at room temperature the same day.

STACY'S PAIRING: Kale chips go well with any beer known to woman, even that sweet pumpkin stuff that pops up every fall. But I think that the best beer to pair with them is a light-bodied ale like Montauk Brewing Company Summer Ale.

1. Place the yogurt, soy sauce, herbs, and salt and pepper in a small mixing bowl and stir to mix them. Cover and refrigerate the dip until you're ready to use it.

2. Garnish the dip with additional herbs right before serving.

Dipping Sauce

⅓ cup plain yogurt

1 teaspoon soy sauce

1 tablespoon freshly chopped tender herbs, such as parsley or chives, plus more for garnish

Sea salt and freshly ground black pepper to taste

Kale Poppers

¼ cup grapeseed oil or other cooking oil

2 tablespoons maple syrup

1 small bunch (about 8 ounces) kale of any variety (larger, fibrous stalks removed), coarsely chopped

1 cup chickpea-fava bean flour

1 teaspoon sea salt

1 teaspoon freshly ground black pepper

1 teaspoon ground mustard

1 teaspoon turmeric powder

To take kale-snacking pleasure to the next level, whip up a batch of these poppers. The chickpea-fava bean flour makes them really luscious. Our local farmers don't grow chickpeas because our climate is too damp. My step-great-grandmother, Angelina Carini—like the good Sicilian she was—grew chickpeas in East Aurora, New York. Both the beans and the leaves are delicious.

Kale, as a member of the cabbage family, should not be used in making stock. You can freeze the stems and later use them, finely chopped, in vegetable soups or in scrambled eggs. —*Stacy*

MAKES 12 POPPERS

1. Place the oil, maple syrup, and kale in a food processor and process until the kale is finely ground, not liquefied. Add the flour, salt, pepper, mustard, and turmeric to the food processor and pulse until thoroughly combined. Cover and allow the mixture to rest for about 10 minutes (or refrigerate for up to 1 day and allow to come to room temperature before baking).

2. Preheat the oven to 400°F. Line a baking sheet with parchment paper.

3. Wet your hands and use them to form the kale mixture, about 2 heaping tablespoons at a time, into 12 balls and place them on the prepared baking sheet.

4. Bake for 10 minutes. Turn the baking sheet around in the oven and bake for about 5 minutes more, until the edges of the poppers turn brown.

5. Serve warm or at room temperature the same day the poppers are baked.

STACY'S PAIRING: A nice, light India pale ale such as Montauk Brewing Company Session IPA complements this snack nicely.

Mile-High Crustless Vegetable Pie

Butter for coating the pan

4 ounces prosciutto, coarsely chopped

5 tablespoons extra virgin olive oil

1 medium Vidalia onion, thinly sliced, then each slice quartered

2 garlic cloves, minced

1 tablespoon sugar

2 medium red potatoes, unpeeled

10 small Brussels sprouts, quartered

1 medium yellow zucchini, unpeeled, ¼-inch slices, diced

8 ounces mushrooms, sliced

½ pint small cherry tomatoes, halved

10 large eggs, at room temperature

¼ cup half-and-half

1 teaspoon sea salt

¾ teaspoon baking powder

¾ pound Gruyère, grated (about 2 cups)

8 ounces cream cheese, chopped

14 fresh basil leaves, tightly packed, finely chopped

2 cups stale baguette cubes

Showcased on elegant Limoges china at a mansion behind the hedges, or on a rough-hewn wooden tray in the backyard, my Mile-High Crustless Vegetable Pie is a happy addition to any table.

No need to go to the gym the day you make this dish—just prepping all the vegetables is a workout, but it's totally worth it. I usually make this impressive mile high pie for lunch or as an appetizer before a light dinner, or to bring to potluck parties. It's generous and hearty, full of flavor, and confidently spreads the love.

Feel free to substitute any, or all, of the vegetables and opt for farm-fresh eggs to raise the result and flavor to a higher level. This pie does not freeze well, so try to finish it the same day you prepare it. —Hillary

SERVES 8

1. Preheat the oven to 350°F. Generously butter the inside of a 10-inch spring-form pan.

2. Fry half the prosciutto in 2 tablespoons of the olive oil over medium heat in a medium frying pan until crisp, about 3 minutes. Remove it from the frying pan and place it in a large bowl.

3. Add the onion and garlic to the frying pan and cook over medium-low heat until translucent, about 3 minutes. Sprinkle with the sugar, turn the heat up, and cook further to caramelize the onions and give them a golden color. Transfer the onion mixture to the bowl with the prosciutto.

4. Slice potatoes into ¼-inch pieces, then quarter.

5. Add 1 tablespoon oil to the pan, heat until hot, add the potatoes, cover, and cook them on high for about 6 minutes, until they are golden and crispy. Add them to the bowl.

6. Add 1 tablespoon oil to the frying pan, heat until hot, add the Brussels sprouts and cook until they are taking on some color, about 4 minutes. Add them to the bowl. Add the raw yellow zucchini to the bowl.

7. Add 1 tablespoon olive oil to the frying pan, heat until hot, add the mushrooms and cook over high heat until they take on color, about 2 minutes. Add them to the bowl. Add the cherry tomatoes and the remaining, uncooked prosciutto to the bowl.

8. Whisk the eggs, half-and-half, salt, and baking powder together in a medium bowl. Stir in the Gruyère, cream cheese, and chopped basil. Add the bread cubes. Pour all of this over the vegetables in the bowl and mix well with your hands.

9. Scoop everything into the springform pan, place the pan on a baking sheet, and put it in the oven to bake for about 1 hour, until firm to the touch at its center.

10. Remove from the oven, allow to rest for 10 minutes, then unmold onto a serving plate. When ready, slice into wedges to serve.

STACY'S PAIRING: Though you want a light, uncomplicated white wine or rosé with this dish, it should have a roundness to counter the dish's eggy complexity. Bridge Lane Rosé offers an almost velvet quality.

Strawberry and Spinach Salad with Chopped Feta Vinaigrette

FOR THE MARINADE

8 ounces feta, coarsely chopped

¼ cup white wine vinegar

⅔ cup grapeseed oil or olive oil

2 tablespoons chopped fresh dill

2 garlic cloves, crushed in a garlic press

2 teaspoons black onion seeds

½ teaspoon ground white pepper

FOR THE SALAD

8 cups (about 5 ounces) baby spinach

½ pint (about 6 ounces) strawberries, hulled and cut in half, if large

¼ cup shelled, salted pumpkin seeds

There's fruit salad and then there's savory fruit salad.

This one works well using any sweet berry or chopped fruit, such as apple, but bright red berries against the deep green spinach really say, "It's almost Christmas in July." The marinated feta can be made in advance and refrigerated for up to a week. Allow it to come to room temperature before using.

This salad makes a great packable lunch when you put a portion into a wide-mouth pint jar with the cheese mixture on the bottom. —Stacy

SERVES 4

1. For the marinade, place the feta, vinegar, oil, dill, garlic, onion seeds, and white pepper together in a sealable container. (I use a quart-size canning jar.) Shake the container to mix the marinade and then allow it to rest at room temperature for 1 hour. Shake it a couple additional times over the course of the hour.

2. To prepare the salad, divide the spinach equally among four salad bowls. Distribute the marinade equally over the four salads. Top each salad with berries and pumpkin seeds.

STACY'S PAIRING: You might look for a crisp, clean-tasting white wine to complement the feta in this dish. Anthony Nappa Wines White Pinot Noir is pink in hue and—surprise!—has a strawberry finish.

Summer Solstice Salad

FOR THE VINAIGRETTE

¾ cup grapeseed oil or extra virgin olive oil

1 teaspoon toasted sesame oil

¼ cup white wine vinegar

1 tablespoon black onion seeds

FOR THE SALAD

4 small fennel bulbs, coarsely chopped

4 large kale leaves, coarsely chopped

1 immature winter squash or a mature kohlrabi, finely sliced

8 ounces purslane

6 squash blossoms

1 pint shelling or sugar snap peas

4 ounces firm goat cheese, crumbled

½ pint fresh raspberries

12 organic nasturtium blossoms for garnish

Basil microgreens for garnish

This is a sort of lazy chopped salad that celebrates what's in season and what's just around the corner. As a gardener, I have access to produce at every stage of its development. I revel in eating shelling peas when their pods are still flat, sweet, and tender; immature winter squash when it's still pale green, yielding something like an avocado in texture; and green fennel seeds. If you don't have access to immature butternut squash for this dish, you can use kohlrabi instead. Calendula petals can be used in place of the squash blossoms or the nasturtiums. —Stacy

SERVES 4

1. For the vinaigrette, place both of the oils, the vinegar, and the onion seeds together in a small, sealable container and shake to mix.

2. To prepare the salad, place the prepared fennel, kale, and squash in a large bowl. Coarsely chop the purslane and add it to the bowl with the prepared vegetables. Gently stir in the vinaigrette and allow the vegetable mixture to rest as you prepare the other salad ingredients.

3. Use a very sharp knife to chop the squash blossoms and pea pods. Gently stir the squash blossoms, peas, cheese, and raspberries into the fennel mixture.

4. Serve in a large salad bowl or 4 medium bowls. Garnish the salad with the nasturtiums and basil microgreens and serve immediately.

STACY'S PAIRING: Look for a very mild white wine like Palmer Vineyards Pinot Blanc. It is a "blanc slate" that allows the intense flavors of the sesame, vinegar, onion seeds, fennel, and cheese to project themselves onto it in concert.

PURSLANE

Purslane is a succulent native to Asia that now grows as a weed all over the world. In the Northeast it seems to favor sprouting up in sidewalk cracks and in planted pots.

Long popular in the cuisines of many countries, purslane is being discovered by Americans and Canadians as more local farmers' markets have taken to selling it.

It's a pretty plant, but one that droops and weeps shortly after being cut—so long-distance shipping is out. Purslane has a mild, lemony flavor and a tender texture when steamed or sautéed. In the late summer, mature purslane drops many small, black seeds, which can be rinsed away.

Purslane is a nutritional powerhouse, but like spinach and rhubarb, it contains oxalates, which are not good for every diet. People taking blood thinners are generally warned to avoid consuming oxalate-rich greens.

I like to serve purslane sautéed as a side for scrambled eggs. Purslane can also be used as a pasta substitute, but in this application it must be very well rinsed after cooking. —*Stacy*

Beet-Stained Potato Salad with Chunky Scallions

FOR THE SALAD

1 medium red onion, finely chopped

One 16-ounce jar pickled sliced beets, finely chopped, brine reserved

4 large russet potatoes, boiled, peeled, finely chopped

½ bunch scallions, sliced into ¼-inch pieces

8 baby sweet pickles, finely chopped

1 cup frozen carrots thawed and drained

1 cup frozen peas, thawed and drained

FOR THE DRESSING

1 tablespoon plus 1 teaspoon apple cider vinegar

1 tablespoon extra virgin olive oil

2 teaspoons sugar

⅓ cup reserved pickled beet brine

1 tablespoon Dijon mustard

3 heaping teaspoons bottled beet horseradish

1½ teaspoons sea salt

6 heaping tablespoons finely chopped fresh dill, plus fronds for garnish

A culinary echo of the famous Russian potato salad, named Olivier Salad and created at the Hermitage Restaurant in Moscow in the late 1800s, my Hamptons version celebrates our potato heritage, then paints in some striking colors and flavors.

Like a veritable flavor factory, it's the kind of salad you keep going back to for another serving, and it keeps delivering. Earthy beets, crunchy pickles, creamy potatoes, chunky scallions, other bits and bobs tossed with an undeniably memorable dressing, and well, it's a keeper, your new favorite salad.

One of my frequent variations is to buy a jar of herring in cream sauce or herring in wine sauce, coarsely chop the herring, then fold it into this bright purple and green salad. —Hillary

SERVES 4 TO 6

1. For the salad, put the onion, beets, potatoes, scallions, pickles, carrots, and peas into a large mixing bowl.

2. To make the dressing, put the vinegar, olive oil, sugar, beet brine, mustard, horseradish, salt, and chopped dill into a bowl and whisk to combine. Pour the dressing over the potato mixture and gently toss to completely coat the vegetables with the dressing.

3. Sprinkle the fronds of dill over the top to decorate. Cover and refrigerate the salad until ready to serve.

STACY'S PAIRING: I searched in vain for just the right locally produced brown ale to accompany this dish. (I hope you have just the right ale where you live— by all means, sample them all.) Locally, I settled on the equation that vinegar plus sugar plus beet brine plus mustard plus horseradish plus dill plus scallions equals Paumanok Vineyards Riesling Semi-Dry Table Wine. It's quite sweet, full, and has a rosy flavor note.

Umami Bomb Bread Salad

I try to get away from my computer as much as I can in order to track local food culture—by interviewing chefs, doing wine tastings, and touring farms. But deadlines happen. I'm sometimes committed to working in the bowels of the Rogers Memorial Library in Southampton all day long. I find that I want two things out of lunch at those times—I want to be good and I want to be bad.

Bread salad has become my go-to. It started because I'd often dash out to the salad bar at Schmidt's Market & Produce in Southampton where I'd quickly fill a container with greens and croutons doused with Caesar dressing. Then I started packing my more gourmet version, detailed here. This bread salad has it all—healthy greens, naughty carbs, cheesy umami, and, at this time of year, the season's first cherry tomatoes. Some days I throw in chickpeas.

If you pack this salad for lunch, keep the tomatoes and dressing together in one container, while keeping the greens and the bread in their own containers, until just before serving. —Stacy

SERVES 4

1. Preheat the oven to 350°F. Line a baking sheet with parchment paper.

2. Toss the bread, Pecorino Romano, and black pepper together in a medium mixing bowl. Drizzle in the oil and toss to coat. Dump the bread mixture onto the prepared baking sheet and flatten it out somewhat. Bake the bread mixture for about 10 minutes, until starting to color. Remove the bread mixture from the oven.

3. Place all the dressing ingredients in a food processor and run on high until emulsified, about 20 seconds.

4. Place the tomatoes and mesclun in a large salad bowl and drizzle them with the dressing. Break the baked bread mixture into chunks and gently fold the cheesy bread into the greens mixture. Serve immediately.

STACY'S PAIRING: A lightly oaked Chardonnay or a dry Chenin Blanc like Pauma-nok Vineyards Chenin Blanc Dry Table Wine works with this salad. But unlike a quietly melding white wine, a bold red wine keeps well without refrigeration. So keep a bottle of a powerful red like Osprey's Dominion Cabernet Sauvignon in your file cabinet for lunching.

FOR THE CHEESY BREAD
2 cups stale French-style bread torn into bite-size pieces
1½ cups grated Pecorino Romano
½ teaspoon freshly ground black pepper
⅓ cup olive oil

FOR THE DRESSING
½ cup finely grated Parmigiano-Reggiano
2 tablespoons apple cider vinegar
1 tablespoon prepared mustard
1 tablespoon Worcestershire sauce
2 teaspoons freshly ground black pepper
2 teaspoons balsamic vinegar
2 garlic cloves, minced

FOR THE SALAD
12 Sun Gold or other cherry tomatoes, halved and drained
8 cups spring mesclun mix

Hamptons Famous Fresh Clam Pie

FOR THE CRUST

Butter for coating the pan

Flour for coating the pan

1½ cups crushed oyster crackers

8 tablespoons (1 stick) unsalted butter, melted

¼ teaspoon freshly ground black pepper

FOR THE FILLING

1 medium yellow onion, minced

8 tablespoons (1 stick) unsalted butter

2 cups raw (or canned) clams, drained and roughly chopped (see Note for reserving liquid)

1 large (about 10 ounces) all-purpose potato, baked or boiled, and roughly chopped (peeled or unpeeled)

1 large egg, slightly beaten

¼ teaspoon dried lovage or celery seed

¼ teaspoon dried sage

¼ teaspoon freshly grated nutmeg

1 cup Italian seasoned bread crumbs

Freshly ground black pepper to taste

Paprika for garnish (optional)

This dish was inspired by the baked clam casserole from the Driver's Seat restaurant in Southampton. I could swear that the original was made of nothing but clams, bread crumbs, butter, butter, and . . . butter. It was a very popular dish, though the restaurant that made it famous is no longer there on Jobs Lane.

Use any combination of clams in this dish. The main thing, as in every clam dish, is to avoid overcooking the clams.

I cut down on the ratio of butter to other ingredients from the original recipe, but kept it very buttery, and added a crust so you can slice this pie up, though it's still pretty messy. Make sure that you never find yourself alone with this dish—you might just eat the whole thing! —Stacy

SERVES 4

1. Preheat the oven to 350°F. Butter and flour the bottom and sides of a 10-inch pie plate.

2. To make the crust, in a medium bowl, stir the cracker crumbs, melted butter, and pepper together. Add 1 tablespoon water at a time (up to 3 tablespoons total) and stir after each addition, just until the mixture begins to stick together. Press the crust mixture evenly onto the bottom and sides of the pie plate. Bake about 10 minutes, until golden brown. Remove the crust from the oven and turn the oven up to 400°F.

3. To prepare the filling, in a small frying pan, sauté the onion in 4 tablespoons of the butter over medium heat until translucent, about 5 minutes. Drain the liquid from the onion and reserve it.

4. Mix the onion, clams, potato, egg, lovage, sage, and nutmeg together in a medium mixing bowl. Place the clam mixture in the crust and level it out.

5. In a small bowl, stir the reserved onion cooking liquid into the bread crumbs to slightly moisten them. Top the clam mixture evenly with the prepared bread crumbs and sprinkle with ground black pepper. Dot the top of the bread crumbs with the remaining 4 tablespoons of the butter.

6. Bake the pie in the oven for about 20 minutes, until the top is golden brown and bubbling. Remove it from the oven and allow it to rest for 5 minutes and sprinkle with paprika, if using, before cutting to serve.

STACY'S PAIRING: A white wine with some acidity, like Wölffer Estate Vineyard Trebbiano, which also lends a touch of fruitiness, works well with this seasoned seafood dish. Alternatively, a sweet and sour ale like Blue Point Brewing Company Beach Plum Gose, which itself contains sea salt and seaweed, works well with this salty clam pie.

Broiled Bluefish with Parmesan Panko Crust

My father often came home with a cooler full of bluefish, cleaned while he was still on the fishing boat, and ready to go into the freezer. Bluefish swim in schools, so when you hit the mother lode, you keep reeling them in. Hence, if lucky, he arrived wearing a tired yet endearing smile, with a lot of bluefish.

I often hear people say that bluefish are oily. I've found, however, that when they are fresh they do not taste oily but rather have a lovely clean-tasting thick flesh that is receptive to myriad preparations. Like Gael Greene described as her practice in the foreword to this book, I also slather my bluefish with mayonnaise, and then bread it, bake it, and finally, broil it. Add an explosive squirt of lemon and it's perfection. —Hillary

SERVES 4

1. Preheat the oven to 500°F. Set a rack 3 to 4 inches below the flame from the broiler. Generously brush a baking sheet with olive oil.

2. In a small bowl, mix together the mayonnaise, mustard, and garlic and set aside.

3. Into another small bowl, add the bread crumbs, salt, pepper, cayenne, parsley, and Parmesan and mix until blended. Pour on the melted butter and massage with your fingers until well blended.

4. Place the bluefish fillets, flesh side up, on the prepared baking sheet. Brush them with the mayonnaise mixture, then pat the bread crumbs over the tops.

5. Bake the fish in the oven for 5 to 12 minutes, depending on the thickness of the fish, until the flesh flakes easily.

6. Turn on the broiler. When the broiler is ready, put the baking sheet under the broiler and cook until the crust on the fillets is golden brown. Serve with the quartered lemons.

2 tablespoons mayonnaise

1 teaspoon Dijon mustard

1 large garlic clove, minced

1 cup Panko bread crumbs

¼ teaspoon sea salt

3 cracks freshly ground black pepper

⅛ teaspoon cayenne pepper

2 tablespoons finely chopped flat-leaf parsley

¼ cup freshly grated Parmesan

2 tablespoons unsalted butter, melted

1½ pounds bluefish, cut into 4 equal pieces

2 lemons, quartered, for serving

STACY'S PAIRING: Seek out a not-too-sweet white wine with some textural complexity for this dish. After some delight-filled explorations, I settled on a rather dry white that sports a heady nose, Kontokosta Winery Viognier.

Blue Cheese Chicken with Strawberry Salsa

10 pieces skinless, organic, bone-in chicken

1 large egg, beaten

½ cup maple syrup

½ cup apple cider vinegar

1 tablespoon kosher salt

½ cup crumbled blue cheese

1 cup fine dried bread crumbs

2 tablespoons all-purpose flour

1 teaspoon freshly ground black pepper

1 teaspoon cornstarch

1 teaspoon ground mustard

1 tablespoon olive oil for coating the baking dish

FOR THE SALSA

1 quart strawberries, hulled and sliced

1 tablespoon balsamic vinegar

1 tablespoon snipped fresh chives

When I was a kid, it was my job to shake pieces of chicken in a bag to help my mom prepare a Shake 'n Bake dinner. I'd like to think I was good at it. I've since perfected my technique using my own shake-then-bake recipe.

This subtly sweet and cheesy chicken dish takes a couple of hours to marinate, so start early. We're dark meat people at my house, so we do all thighs and drumsticks. If you double this recipe, prepare two bags of the coating mix separately. Ten pieces of chicken are about all one paper bag can stand up to.

Serve hot or warm. This dish packs well for a picnic. —*Stacy*

SERVES 4

1. Place the chicken pieces in a 9-by-13-inch baking dish.

2. Whisk the egg, maple syrup, vinegar, and salt together in a small bowl with a fork. Pour the marinade over the chicken. Cover loosely with waxed paper and marinate in the refrigerator for about 2 hours, turning the chicken pieces over after the first hour.

3. Meanwhile, preheat the oven to 200°F. Line a baking sheet with parchment paper.

4. Place the crumbled blue cheese on the prepared sheet and heat it in the oven for 1 hour. The cheese should be golden. Remove the pan from the oven and place the parchment paper covered with cheese on a cooling rack to rest until the cheese is room temperature. Run the cooled cheese through a food processor (or blender) for about 20 seconds to make it into pieces that resemble Panko crumbs. This process cannot be rushed. You're making the cheese into a crumble so that it can adhere in a fairly uniform, somewhat crunchy layer.

5. To make the coating, mix together the bread crumbs, flour, pepper, cornstarch, and mustard by placing them in a paper lunch bag. Hold the bag closed and shake it a few times to mix the coating. Just before you're about to start coating the pieces of chicken, you'll add the crumbled blue cheese to the bag and shake it once.

6. Preheat the oven to 400°F.

7. Coat the bottom of the baking dish with the oil.

8. Remove the chicken pieces from the marinade, allowing any excess marinade to drip off. Dredge the chicken pieces by placing them in the bag, one at a time, and shaking the closed bag a few times. Arrange the chicken pieces in the prepared dish and bake for about 45 minutes, until the chicken's internal temperature reaches 165°F on an instant-read thermometer.

9. To prepare the salsa, place the strawberries in a medium mixing bowl. Drizzle the vinegar on the berries and then sprinkle them with the chives. Gently stir to combine.

10. Serve the chicken hot, or at room temperature, with the salsa on the side.

STACY'S PAIRING: I recommend Merlot with this unusual meat dish. For instance, if Bedell Cellars Merlot could speak, it would say, "Merlot, I'm a medium-bodied red with a touch of berry flavor." And it works well with this cheesed chicken dish. Though Palmer Vineyards Merlot, with its leathery dark fruit notes, also works particularly well given the slight sweetness of the maple syrup.

Long Island Duck Breasts with Duck Walk Vineyards Blueberry Port Sauce

FOR THE SAUCE

½ yellow onion

1½ cups fresh blueberries, plus more for garnish

¼ cup plus 2 tablespoons light brown sugar

1¼ cups Duck Walk Vineyards Blueberry Port

2 tablespoons apple cider vinegar

½ teaspoon allspice

½ teaspoon sea salt

2 tablespoons unsalted butter

FOR THE DUCK

16 ounces pappardelle pasta or wide egg noodles

1 tablespoon olive oil or butter

4 Long Island duck breasts

Fine sea salt and freshly ground black pepper to taste

Rosemary for garnish

My French friend Helene was visiting the Hamptons for a long weekend. I had tried to introduce her to American food, fried clam bellies and lobster rolls, at a joint on the way to Montauk; those amazing jelly-filled croissants they make at the Montauk Bake Shoppe; clam chowder at Bostwick's Chowder House, and she had loved it all. Now she wanted to make "that dish with cherries and duck" that I had cooked in France, but this time with the most fragrant Hamptons blueberries.

Still wanting to share what I love so much about living here, I piled her into the car and drove her a couple of miles down the road to Duck Walk Vineyards. I knew they had a blueberry port that would work wonders with this recipe. They poured her a taste, and that questioning smile turned into a knowing grin.

This super easy recipe that she was referring to is reminiscent of an old-fashioned dish that I used to make in France, called Duck Montmorency. Here in the Hamptons, I now make it with blueberries and a blueberry port from just a couple of miles down the road. The next day, Helene bought a few bottles of blueberry port to take home. —*Hillary*

SERVES 4

1. To make the sauce, put the onion in a food processor and finely chop. Scoop the onion into a medium saucepan. Add the blueberries, sugar, blueberry port, vinegar, allspice, and salt. Bring the mixture to a boil. Reduce to a simmer, cover, and cook for 15 minutes. Whisk well and then keep warm.

2. Cook the pasta according to package instructions, toss in the olive oil, and keep warm.

3. Preheat the oven to 400°F.

4. Place the duck breasts on a cutting board, skin side down. With a rolling pin, hit each breast to flatten a little. Turn them over and, with a small sharp knife, make diagonal cuts on their skin to create a diamond pattern. Rub all over with salt and pepper.

5. Heat a large iron or ovenproof frying pan over medium-high heat until very hot. Add the duck breasts, skin side down, and cook for about 3 minutes. Careful not to spatter, pour off the duck fat (save it for another use), and place the frying pan in the hot oven for 10 to 12 minutes, until an instant-read thermometer in the duck reads 160°F. Flip over the breasts and cook another minute, then take them out of the oven and reserve until ready to serve.

6. To serve, reheat the sauce over medium-high heat for just 1 minute, and whisk in the 2 tablespoons butter until melted and the sauce is glossy. Slice the duck breasts across the grain into ½-inch slices. Mound the pasta on each plate, arrange duck slices in a fan to the side. Drizzle the blueberry sauce around the duck and garnish with fresh blueberries and rosemary.

STACY'S PAIRING: You want to find a fun, fruity wine to work with the sweet blueberry, rich duck, and hit of allspice in this dish. Laurel Lake Vineyards Moscato Sparkling Wine pairs well with this unique combination of flavors.

Steak Picnic Sandwiches with Whole Cherry Tomato Jam

FOR THE JAM
2 pints cherry tomatoes
2 tablespoons olive oil
1 cup sugar
⅓ cup dark brown sugar
½ cup fruity red wine
1 teaspoon apple cider
 vinegar
½ teaspoon sea salt

FOR THE SANDWICHES
2 pounds flank steak, at
 room temperature
2 tablespoons olive oil
Sea salt and freshly ground
 black pepper to taste
1 large baguette or 4 small
 ones

Leftover jam can be refrigerated in a sealed container for use within 1 week.

The beach parking lot was crammed with pickup trucks packed with surfboards and fishing gear. And there were drums on the ground. And baskets of food. And barefoot children carrying folded blankets walking up the sandy path toward the beach.

I was filled with excitement. I had always wanted to go to the Drum Circle on Sagg Main Beach, a weekly summer event that draws surfers, babies, babes, surf casters, and lots of drums.

The sun was setting a glorious peach and lavender. It turned out to be all about everything. The music. The sunset. The dancing and laughing. Hula-Hoops and dogs. And, inevitably, it was also about food. A great excuse to bring a picnic and chill.

I brought friends with me and made this easy-to-pack and easy-to-serve dinner. It's a no-brainer. Simply wrap the sliced steak in foil that's lined with parchment paper. Pre-slice the baguette and wrap it separately in brown paper, or parchment, and twine. (I use long-fermented wheat baguettes from Carissa's the Bakery, or her pickle juice rye bread that's made with locally grown rye, fresh from her store in East Hampton.) Carry the jam in a Mason jar with a lid. Put it all in a basket with an easy dessert, and you're ready to go drumming. —Hillary

SERVES 4

1. Make the jam in two steps. First, preheat the oven to 350°F and line a baking pan with parchment paper. Toss the cherry tomatoes in 2 tablespoons of olive oil to thoroughly coat, place them on the baking pan, and bake for 45 minutes. They will come out looking wrinkly. Cool to room temperature.

2. For the second step, add the sugars, wine, vinegar, and salt into a small saucepan. Bring to a boil, reduce to a simmer, and cook down until the mixture is reduced by half and is thickened and sticky. Stir once in a while, but you don't have to stand over it. It should take about 1 hour and 15 minutes.

3. Stir in half the roasted cherry tomatoes, mashing some until the seeds and juices come out. Bring the mixture back to a boil, reduce the heat to medium-high, and cook until the bubbles begin to get smaller and smaller and the jam is thick, about 10 to 12 minutes. Stir in the rest of the cherry

tomatoes and cool to room temperature. It should make 1½ cups of jam. Scoop the jam into a jar with a lid to take on the picnic.

4. Preheat the grill to high. Pat the steak very dry then rub it all over with 2 tablespoons of olive oil and generously season both sides with salt and pepper. Grill for 4 minutes on each side for rare. Cooking it longer may cause the meat to toughen. Allow the meat to rest for 10 minutes before thinly slicing it against the grain. Wrap it up in parchment paper then aluminum foil to take on the picnic.

5. Slice the baguette lengthwise, then slice it into 8 pieces. Wrap it up in parchment or brown paper and twine to take on the picnic.

6. To serve, divide the steak between the pieces of baguette and top with the cherry tomato jam.

STACY'S PAIRING: For this meat-and-tomatoes dish you want a red wine that's not too tannic, but also not too fruity. You'll find that in Cabernet Franc. I particularly like Bedell Cellars and Lieb Cellars Cabernet Francs for outings with this sandwich in tow.

SAGAPONACK'S ARTISANAL POTATO CHIPS

My favorite potato chips come from the Foster farm stand on Sagg Main Street in Sagaponack. The Foster family grows Peter Wilcox potatoes, peels them, slices them, kettle cooks them, bags them, and sells them out front at the stand. Stop by and pick up a bag or two of their Tiger Spuds Potato Chips. Thick, cooked in good quality oil, lightly salted, and totally crunch-worthy, these chips alone should make this farm stand your regular stop. Also ask about the Fosters' farm-to-bottle hyper-local potato and wheat vodkas, called Sagaponacka Vodka, which they produce in their Sagaponack Farm Distillery. —Hillary

Strawberry Sour Cream Ice Cream

The month of June is strawberry season, when I pick my own. It's a short road trip to the nearest strawberry patch. While I am filling my basket, I am thinking of things to make with them, like chocolate-dipped strawberries, strawberry pie, or strawberry scones. But then, with the sun warming my back and the temperature rising, all is swept away for the idea of making a luscious strawberry ice cream with fresh strawberries on the side. It can be ready in time for dinner with minimal work.

I like to serve strawberry ice cream with freshly chopped strawberries and a bowl of whipped cream. There's nothing like strawberries with more cream on top of your ice cream!

I introduce a twist by adding sour cream for a tangy hit of flavor, and I also add vodka when making ice cream, as vodka lowers the freezing point and helps eliminate ice crystals. When I serve this, I marinate the chopped strawberries in strawberry vodka and offer them in a bowl on the side. —Hillary

MAKES ABOUT 1 PINT

1. Clean and hull the strawberries. Toss them into the bowl of a food processor and process until smooth. Add the rest of the ingredients and process until the sugar is dissolved and the mixture is very smooth.

2. Chill in the refrigerator for 4 hours.

3. Add the mixture to your ice cream maker and churn until thick. Scoop into a freezer container and place in the freezer to harden. If you don't have an ice cream maker, pour the mixture into a loaf pan lined with parchment paper, cover, and freeze. When ready to serve, take out of the freezer and allow to rest at room temperature for 10 minutes, then scoop into bowls.

STACY'S PAIRING: A Cabernet Franc, tannic and dry, like Raphael's Cabernet Franc provides a bright, bitey contrast to sweet, cold strawberries. Its tannins cut through the cream and remind you that everything you eat and drink is alive. It even seems to bring a touch of heat.

16 ounces fresh strawberries

2 cups sour cream

1 cup heavy whipping cream

1 cup sugar

3 tablespoons strawberry vodka

3 tablespoons strawberry jam

1 teaspoon pure vanilla extract

1 teaspoon fresh lemon juice

⅛ teaspoon sea salt

Cherry Sweet Cheese Pocket Pies

FOR THE CRUST

2½ cups flour

½ pound (2 sticks) unsalted butter, at room temperature

⅛ teaspoon kosher salt

1 large egg, beaten, for painting the dough

FOR THE FILLING

¼ cup sugar

½ cup cherry jam

1 cup (7.5 ounces) farmer cheese

2 tablespoons cornstarch

1 teaspoon white balsamic vinegar

¼ teaspoon ground cinnamon

⅛ teaspoon freshly grated nutmeg

STACY'S PAIRING: A shot of vodka that has a touch of sweetness in one hand, like Sagaponacka Wheat Vodka, is a nice complement to the pocket pie in your other hand.

My family has always made every kind of pie, including hand pies, which you can eat with one hand while you do chores. After I moved to Sag Harbor, local fisherman Al "Big Time" Daniels set me straight. What I called hand pies are "pocket pies," because you stick them in your pocket before you go out fishing or hunting.

Al's mother was famous for her delicious pocket pies. She squeezed the pits from hundreds of beach plums to make a batch. Al tells me that she swore by using butter-flavored Crisco in her crust. I prefer to use a classic butter crust, because I find it offers the necessary strength and flakiness. These pies are best served warm.

You can use just about any jam you like, and you can use ricotta in place of the farmer cheese. —*Stacy*

MAKES 6 POCKET PIES

1. Preheat the oven to 400°F. Line two baking sheets with parchment paper.

2. To prepare the crust, place the flour, butter, and salt in the bowl of a stand mixer and mix with a pastry knife by hand until the butter is in pebble-sized chunks. Add 6 tablespoons cold water and mix with the stand mixer on medium speed until the dough is uniform and just holding together, about 30 seconds, scraping down the sides of the bowl and beater as needed.

3. To make the filling, in a small mixing bowl, mix the sugar, jam, cheese, cornstarch, vinegar, cinnamon, and nutmeg together. Set aside.

4. Roll out the dough on a floured surface to about ¼-inch thick. Cut the dough into six 6-inch disks and place them on the prepared baking sheets.

5. Crack the egg into a cup and whisk vigorously with a fork. Use a pastry brush to paint the egg along half the edge of each circle. Place 2 heaping tablespoons of filling on the egged half of each circle. Fold the discs in half, so that the "dry" edge meets the egged edge, and crimp them together with a fork to seal. Use the fork to perforate the top crust at the center of each pocket pie once. Bake the pies about 30 minutes, until golden brown.

Red Berry Pudding in Mason Jars

½ cup fine cornmeal

3 cups whole milk

2 cups heavy cream

½ cup sugar

1 pint red raspberries

1 pint strawberries

FOR THE SYRUP (OPTIONAL)

1 tablespoon red wine

¼ cup confectioners' sugar

This type of corn pudding is considered an English dessert. Dairy cows were unknown in North America before Europeans arrived, after all. Corn pudding was widely consumed by Native Americans and by colonists. Long Island corn pudding is called samp, and it was enjoyed by locals well into the 20th century.

Because refrigeration zaps flavor and dries out delicate produce, buy freshly picked berries and use them quickly to avoid refrigeration whenever possible. The best fruit and vegetables still hold a touch of sun heat when you start to cook with them. Rinse and dry fresh berries just before you use them.

If you have sweet cherries in your local farmers' market, feel free to use them in place of some, or all, of the red berries. —*Stacy*

MAKES 8 PUDDINGS

1. Stir the cornmeal into 1 cup of the milk and set the mixture aside.

2. Stir together the cream, 2 cups of the milk, and the sugar in a medium saucepan. Bring the cream mixture just to a boil. Add the cornmeal mixture to the saucepan and whisk to combine. Whisking continuously, cook just below boiling until the pudding has thickened and the cornmeal has softened, about 10 minutes.

3. Using a canning funnel, fill eight half-pint Mason jars a bit more than half full with pudding. Allow the pudding to cool to room temperature. Then cover the jars and refrigerate to chill for at least 30 minutes.

4. When ready to serve, or to pack for a picnic, hull the strawberries and slice the larger berries. Place all the berries together in a medium mixing bowl.

5. For the syrup, if using, drizzle the berries with the red wine, sprinkle with the confectioners' sugar, and stir gently.

6. Use a slotted spoon to cover the puddings with berries. Serve with small spoons for dipping into the jars.

Any leftover berries and syrup should be enjoyed in your next fresh fruit salad or ice cream sundae.

STACY'S PAIRING: Savor a glass of your favorite Cabernet Franc or port after enjoying a jar (or two) of this pudding. Bordo Antico, a Cabernet Franc from North Fork winemaker Anthony Nappa, also works very well with this rich treat.

Swiss Chard and Sag Harbor Rum Pie with Rum Custard Sauce

FOR THE CUSTARD SAUCE

4 large egg yolks, at room temperature

¼ cup sugar

¼ teaspoon sea salt

2 cups milk or almond milk or cream

3 tablespoons Sag Harbor Rum or other spiced rum

1 teaspoon pure vanilla extract

FOR THE PIECRUST

2½ cups flour

2 tablespoons sugar

½ teaspoon sea salt

¼ teaspoon baking powder

½ teaspoon ground cinnamon

½ pound (2 sticks) unsalted butter, cubed

1 egg beaten with 1 tablespoon water for an egg wash

Olive oil to grease springform pan

Early on in my years living in a village near Nice in the south of France, I became fascinated with a sweet Swiss chard pie, called *la tourte de blettes,* which was sold by the slice in open air markets. It was thin and had a top crust, and the inside was a mixture of Swiss chard, pine nuts, freshly made candied fruits, and rum. It was addictive, and because I miss it, I make a version of it here.

Since freshly made candied fruits, like the ones used in the south of France, are not readily available, I have adapted my original recipe to use ingredients I can find in the Hamptons. Happily, I discovered that it is even better made with hazelnuts and local rum, plus a gorgeous draping of rum custard sauce. My favored rum for this dish is Old Whalers Style Sag Harbor Hand Crafted Rum, with its subtle flavors of fruits and spices. *—Hillary*

MAKES ONE 10-INCH PIE

1. To make the custard sauce, put the 4 egg yolks and ¼ cup sugar in a medium mixing bowl and whisk vigorously until the mixture is pale and smooth. Whisk in the ¼ teaspoon salt.

2. Bring the milk to a boil in a medium saucepan. Take off the heat and gradually whisk the hot milk into the eggs, then pour all of this back into the saucepan and whisk over low heat until it turns into a thickened custard, 10 to 12 minutes. Remove from the heat, whisk in the rum and vanilla, then allow to cool to room temperature. Cover and refrigerate until ready to use.

3. Make the piecrusts by adding the flour, 2 tablespoons sugar, ½ teaspoon salt, baking powder, and cinnamon to the bowl of a food processor and pulsing six times. Add the cubed butter and pulse 15 times, until it looks mealy. Then, with the machine running, pour in 4 tablespoons cold water and process. Pinch the dough to see if it comes together. If not, add an additional tablespoon of water and process.

4. Scoop the dough out onto a large piece of parchment paper and use your hands to bring the dough together into a ball. Slice it in half, wrap each half in parchment paper, and refrigerate for 1 hour.

5. Meanwhile, make the filling. Soak the raisins in the rum for 30 minutes.

6. Remove the stalks from the Swiss chard and wash and dry the leaves. Roll the leaves and slice them vertically into ¼-inch strips to yield about 4 tightly packed cups of chard. Reserve.

7. Preheat the oven to 375°F.

8. Into a large bowl, add the raisins, rum, brown sugar, hazelnuts, 2 eggs, 1 tablespoon olive oil, ½ teaspoon salt, and orange zest and mix well with your hands. Add the Swiss chard leaves and mix again.

9. Line the bottom of a 10-inch springform pan with parchment paper cut to fit and grease with olive oil. Take one piece of dough from the refrigerator. Roll it out on a clean floured surface into a circle big enough to fit the bottom of the springform pan and at least halfway up the sides. Fit it into the pan. Pour in the filling and pat down with a spatula.

10. Roll out the second piece of dough to fit over the top of the pie with a little to spare. Lay it over the top of the filling and gently press down around the edges and against the walls of the pan to seal the two piecrusts together. Gently roll over the dough edges around the perimeter to create a stand-up crust, and then use your fingers to pinch it into a ruffled shape.

11. With a pastry brush, paint the top of the crust with the egg wash, and make 2 small knife slits in the center to allow steam to escape.

12. Place the springform pan on a baking sheet, put it into the oven and bake for 35 to 45 minutes, until golden brown.

13. Meanwhile, take the custard out of the refrigerator to come to room temperature.

14. Remove the pie from the oven and allow it to rest for 10 minutes before releasing the spring, transferring the pie to a serving plate, and serving each slice with a generous draping of custard sauce.

STACY'S PAIRING: A round of Old Whalers Style Sag Harbor Hand Crafted Rum, or another spiced rum, is in order.

FOR THE PIE FILLING
6 tablespoons raisins
2 ounces Sag Harbor Rum or other spiced rum
2 pounds Swiss chard
¼ cup light brown sugar
½ cup chopped hazelnuts
2 eggs, beaten
1 tablespoon olive oil
½ teaspoon salt
½ organic orange, zested

Chapter Three

HIGH SUMMER

Fourth of July to Labor Day

High summer explodes in a riot of warm-weather produce
at its peak. This chapter provides recipes and inspiration
for using this abundant harvest, with an emphasis
on outdoor grilling.

Corn and Lobster Chowder

6 ears fresh corn, shucked

Two 1½-pound lobsters, cooked

3 tablespoons extra virgin olive oil

3 medium shallots, finely diced

5 tablespoons flour

1 teaspoon sea salt

1 teaspoon ground turmeric

2 ears fresh corn

2 large potatoes, cooked, sliced in chunks

1 medium orange bell pepper, finely diced

½ teaspoon paprika

¾ cup minced fresh parsley

My friend was walking up the driveway carrying two 3-pound (at least) live lobsters, one wiggling in each hand. He was smiling.

That afternoon we created an amazing lobster chowder using the local sweet corn I had just bought that morning from Pike Farms, down the road on Sagg Main Street. I let him cook the lobsters while I played around with the corn. Instead of taking a traditional approach in using cream in the evolving soup, I chose to make a quick corn milk, then thicken it a bit with some flour.

On his side of the kitchen, my friend had a huge deep pot roiling with boiling water. He deftly dropped each lobster in, head first, and timed them for 7 minutes. Using tongs, he took each one out and ran it under cold running water to cool them down.

Sharing in the creation of this dish with an old friend was as much fun as discovering how utterly delicious it turned out. You have to try it. If you are squeamish about cooking lobsters, ask the fish store to cook them for you. I scrape off fresh summer corn kernels into containers to freeze so that I can make this in the winter as well. —*Hillary*

SERVES 4

1. Shave the raw corn kernels off 3 ears of corn into a food processor. Add 3 cups water and process until milky. The mixture will still have texture from the corn kernels. Pour it into a large bowl. Repeat with the remaining 3 ears of corn and additional 3 cups water.

2. Remove the claws from the lobsters and reserve. Remove the lobster tail meat and slice each tail in half vertically so that you have four slices of lobster tail, one for each bowl. Reserve. Take any other meat and lobster juice out of the lobsters and reserve.

3. Heat the olive oil in a large saucepan over medium-low heat. Add the shallots and cook until they are soft, about 4 minutes. Sift in the flour evenly over the top and stir until well coated. Add the corn milk, bring to a boil, and simmer while whisking until the soup thickens, 3 to 5 minutes. Add the salt and turmeric and stir to blend.

4. Shave kernels off 2 ears of corn and stir them into the soup.

Continued . . .

5. Add the chunks of cooked potato, bell pepper, paprika, and ½ cup of the parsley. Add any reserved lobster liquid and all lobster meat except the four claws. Stir to combine.

6. To serve, divide the chowder between the four bowls. Add one claw to the center of each bowl. Garnish each bowl with the remaining minced parsley and serve.

STACY'S PAIRING: A sparkling wine such as Wölffer Estate Vineyard Noblesse Oblige Brut Rosé is ideal with this rich, flavorful dish. Though a still, well-balanced Chardonnay with a full palate like Martha Clara Vineyards Estate Reserve Chardonnay works admirably to amplify the natural sweetness of the lobster and corn in this dish.

LONG ISLAND LOBSTERS

There are few local Long Island lobsters to be had these days—so if you find some, know that they are very special indeed. Most lobsters served on Long Island are from Maine or Canada. Long Island Sound lobsters suffered a huge die-off in 1999 that has been linked to pesticide use at that time. And warming ocean water temperatures are driving lobsters farther north. That said, lobsters are a big part of a Hamptons summer, being served in lobster rolls, at clambakes, and at iconic restaurants.

Buy your lobsters fresh on the day you wish to cook them. Ask when they arrived at the store, those in tanks can be days old. Take a good look at them and pick ones that are lively and have their tails curling under their bodies. Once home, keep them in damp paper towels in the refrigerator until you are ready to cook them. Do not put them in tap water in your sink as they will die and the meat will become mushy when you cook them.

To boil lobsters, fill a stockpot with liberally salted water (2 tablespoons salt for each gallon of water) and bring it to a roiling boil. You should be able to cook two lobsters at a time. Holding the lobsters by their bodies with potholders, quickly plunge them head first into the boiling water and cover the pot. If you are going to add them to a recipe and cook them further, cook them for 3 to 5 minutes, until they have just turned red.

If serving them on their own, cook them for 8 minutes. For lobsters larger than 1½ pounds, increase the cooking time to about 10 to 13 minutes. Note that in the winter, lobsters have harder shells, so the cooking time may be a bit longer.

Use tongs to pull them out of the boiling water directly into a colander. Because the lobsters will continue to cook in the shell, and you don't want them overcooked, place the colander in the sink under cold running water to cool them down and stop the cooking.

If you are cooking lobsters and corn for the same meal, they cook about the same amount of time so it is easy to set up two stockpots next to each other on the stove, bring both to a roiling boil, drop the lobsters into one pot and drop the corn into the other pot. Lobsters and corn can come out after about 8 minutes. —Hillary

Seared Tuna

This is a very popular starter on Long Island's East End. If you can find whole yellow and brown mustard seeds where you live, you can use them instead of sesame seeds for an added pop of flavor and crunch. The tuna is cooked just enough to give it a caramelized outer layer, while the inside stays pink. —Stacy

SERVES 4

Grapeseed oil
Soy sauce
½ cup white sesame seeds
½ cup black sesame seeds
1 pound sushi-grade tuna
   steak
Sesame oil for drizzling
Chives, freshly snipped, for
   garnish (optional)

1. Pour oil to a depth of ¼ inch in a large, heavy frying pan. Heat over high heat until the oil shimmers.

2. Meanwhile, pour a shallow pool of soy sauce on the serving plate. Line another large plate with paper towels.

3. Mix all the seeds together in a small bowl.

4. Cut the tuna into 1-inch strips. Cut the strips into 1-inch cubes. Press the cubes into the seeds to coat them, one at a time, on all sides. Fry the prepared tuna for 45 seconds. Turn the pieces of tuna over and fry for an additional 45 seconds. Remove the cooked tuna to the paper towel–lined plate to drain for a few seconds and drizzle them with sesame oil.

5. Place the seared tuna pieces in the pool of soy sauce, on the serving plate, and sprinkle them with the chives, if using. Serve immediately.

STACY'S PAIRING: The very light hoppiness of an American amber lager like Blue Point Brewing Company's Toasted Lager works well with this fish dish. This particular beer also offers an echo of toasty caramelization.

Summer Succotash

FOR THE SUCCOTASH

4 slices bacon

1 medium yellow onion, chopped

2 garlic cloves, crushed in a garlic press

1 red bell pepper, chopped

1 cup sweet corn kernels (about 2 ears)

1 small summer squash, chopped

2 cups fresh beans such as fava, edamame, or lima

1 pint (about 6 ounces) small okra pods, chopped

½ cup vegetable stock

1 teaspoon dried marjoram

1 teaspoon kosher salt

½ teaspoon freshly ground black pepper

1 bay leaf

2 tablespoons chopped fresh dill (or 2 teaspoons dried)

1 tablespoon apple cider vinegar

1 large tomato, chopped

4 scallions for garnish (optional)

FOR THE BREAD CRUMB TOPPING (OPTIONAL)

3 cups dried bread crumbs

8 tablespoons (1 stick) unsalted butter, melted

Succotash is considered a Southern specialty by many, but it actually comes to us from the Narragansett people of Rhode Island. I like to make this filling dish when okra and the three sisters—corn, beans, and squash—are available fresh, at the height of their season. But you can use frozen corn and beans, as well as frozen okra, in this recipe.

I cut the ears of corn in half crosswise before slicing off the kernels; it makes the slicing easier.

This recipe can also make a hearty main dish for four, when served over riced cauliflower. —Stacy

SERVES 6

1. Preheat the oven to 400°F.

2. Spread the bacon slices in the bottom of a Dutch oven and cover them loosely with parchment paper. Bake in the oven until the bacon is slightly crispy, about 15 minutes. Remove the Dutch oven from the oven to a burner over medium heat, leaving the oven on. Remove the bacon slices from the pot and set them aside. Add the onions to the fat in the pot and fry them until they start to brown, about 5 minutes, stirring frequently.

3. Add the garlic and red bell pepper to the pot and fry for about 3 minutes to soften the pepper.

4. Add the corn, squash, beans, okra, stock, marjoram, salt, pepper, bay leaf, and dill to the pot and stir to mix. Cover the mixture and allow it to steam until the vegetables are tender, about 12 minutes. Remove the bay leaf.

5. Chop the bacon. Stir the bacon, vinegar, and tomato into the vegetable mixture.

6. To serve at room temperature, portion the mixture into six 5-inch ramekins. Top with 4 fresh, chopped scallions and serve.

7. To serve hot, portion the mixture into six 5-inch ramekins. Mix the bread crumbs and butter together and cover each ramekin of succotash with the bread crumb mixture. Place the ramekins on a sturdy baking sheet. Heat the succotash in the ramekins in the 400°F oven until the tops have crisped, about 10 minutes, and serve.

STACY'S PAIRING: Go for a light ale with just a touch of sweetness, one that doesn't try to compete with the dill in this dish—like Montauk Brewing Company Summer Ale.

FAVA BEANS

People who have experienced the joys of fava beans (also called "broad beans")—that velvety texture and pronounced sweetness—can't get enough of them. If you're a fava bean newbie, yes, you must peel them twice. After removing the beans from their hairy pods, you must then score them with your fingernail, or a paring knife, and peel the individual beans. —Stacy

Stuffed Clams in Shells from the Beach

The best shell shopping happens after a storm. A walk along the beach in the morning yields treasure. Your pockets start to fill with souvenirs of sea glass and shells that have tumbled their way from afar to this very beach. They're free and each one is unique, like a snowflake. Soon you have a whole tote bag filled with these beauties. The sea glass will go into craft-making. The shells can be used to hold seafood, if they are big enough.

To use found shells for cooking, clean them well in soapy water or run them through the dishwasher. Stuff and bake them, using this recipe, for an appetizer that pairs well with a seafood dinner after a storm. —Hillary

SERVES 4

1. Preheat the oven to 350°F.

2. Scrub the clams under cold running water, discarding any that are open.

3. Pour the clam juice into a large frying pan, add the clams, cover, and steam until they have just opened. The time required will depend on the size of the clams.

4. Once opened, remove the clams from the broth and coarsely chop them. Reserve the broth.

5. Heat the olive oil and 4 tablespoons butter in a medium pot over medium heat. Add the shallot and garlic, and cook, stirring frequently, until they are tender, about 3 minutes.

6. Add the oregano, bread, cheese, lemon juice, bell pepper, salt, cayenne, and parsley and stir to mix. Add enough of the reserved clam broth to the mixture and stir until it comes together to make a moist stuffing.

7. Stuff the clam shells with the mixture, brush the tops with the melted butter, then dust each with paprika. Place on a rimmed baking sheet and bake for 25 minutes, until they are golden brown, then serve.

STACY'S PAIRING: A dry but fruity Sauvignon Blanc like Kontokosta Winery Sauvignon Blanc works well with this dish. Or try a light-bodied lager like Southampton Publick House Southampton Light.

12 cherrystone clams
1 cup bottled clam juice
2 tablespoons extra virgin olive oil
8 tablespoons (1 stick) unsalted butter (4 tablespoons of it melted)
1 large shallot, minced
4 garlic cloves, minced
1 teaspoon minced fresh oregano
4 cups finely diced stale white bread
2 tablespoons Pecorino Romano, finely grated
½ lemon, juiced
1 small red bell pepper, finely diced
¼ teaspoon sea salt
⅛ teaspoon cayenne pepper
3 tablespoons minced fresh parsley
Paprika for dusting

Grilled Shishito Peppers

1 quart (about 9 ounces) whole shishito or Padrón peppers
¼ cup extra virgin olive oil
½ teaspoon Amagansett Sea Salt or other finishing salt

Blackened shishito peppers have been very popular in Hamptons restaurants for the last 10 years. You can easily prepare them at home. Legend has it that one out of 10 shishito peppers is very hot, while the rest are quite mild. I find that hot ones occur less frequently than that, but the fact that they look exactly like all the others makes for an ongoing game of roulette. For a touch more heat in general, use Padrón peppers instead of shishito. —*Stacy*

SERVES 6

TO GRILL:

1. Set up the grill for direct grilling and preheat to high.

2. These small, thin-walled peppers can be prepared on the grill by threading them onto skewers and grilling over high heat for about 2 minutes and then turning them over for 2 minutes more, until they're blistered all over.

3. To serve, use a large fork to push the peppers off of the skewers and onto a large serving platter. Drizzle them with the olive oil and season with the salt.

TO DRY FRY:

1. Heat a cast-iron frying pan over high heat until smoking hot, about 5 minutes.

2. Place all the peppers in the pan and heat them for about 3 minutes, turn them over with a spatula and cook for 3 minutes more. Turn them once more after this and cook them until they're blistered all over, for 1 to 2 additional minutes.

3. To serve, transfer the peppers to a large serving plate, drizzle with olive oil, and season with the salt.

STACY'S PAIRING: Beer and plenty of it. Look for a light lager with a balanced malty sweetness and a touch of toastiness. For now, I've settled on Oyster Bay Brewing Company Classic American Lager, but my search continues for more options.

SUMMER VEGETABLE GRILLING TIPS

Many vegetables can be easily grilled. Just slice up the big ones, leave the small ones whole, paint them with oil, and salt and pepper to taste. Most require just a couple minutes on each side to cook through.

- You might choose to oven roast or parboil large, dense vegetables like potatoes and beets before grilling them.
- Some vegetables require a little extra help, like asparagus. You can try your luck at grilling spears across the grate of the grill, but why not play it safe and make a "raft" by inserting three evenly spaced skewers through about six spears at a time?
- Remember to soak bamboo skewers in water for about 30 minutes before using them on the grill—to prevent them from catching on fire. —Stacy

Corn on the Cob

½ cup kosher salt

12 ears corn

Butter

Sea salt

Leftover corn can be cut from the cob and frozen for up to 6 months. Organic corn silk can be dried for use as a tea.

My Grandma Arlene was still a skinny little thing after she had her first child, my Aunt Anita. So, it came as quite a surprise to people who didn't know her when she won a corn-on-the-cob eating contest in Little Valley, New York. Her husband, Pop-pop John, was not surprised. Corn and butter were two of her favorite foods. She ate 15 ears that day.

Speaking of well-meaning exertions, I once read a recipe for corn-on-the-cob that recommended putting unshucked ears of corn in a burlap bag and throwing it as far as you could into the ocean 11 times to season it before cooking it on the beach. Okay, I haven't actually tried this method, but it can't be necessary.

My method produces a steamed kernel with a hint of the grill. Alternatively, you can shuck and oil the ears of corn before placing them on the grill. Cooked this way, the corn is cooked and blackened very quickly. —Stacy

SERVES 6

1. Place about a gallon of cold water in a 3-gallon stockpot and stir in the salt until it has dissolved.

2. Open the cornhusks, but do not remove them. Remove as much of the corn silk from the corn as you can. Close the husks back up and place all of the ears of corn upright in the pot to soak. Add more cold water so that the ears are submerged. Allow the corn to rest for at least 1 hour.

3. Set up the grill for direct grilling and preheat to high.

4. Remove the ears from the pot and allow them to drain well before grilling. Place the ears on the grill, close the cover, and grill until the kernels are tender when pierced with a paring knife, about 15 to 20 minutes, turning every 5 minutes.

5. Remove the ears from the grill and peel back the husks, but do not remove them. Braid the husks to form built-in handles. Serve immediately with butter and sea salt.

STACY'S PAIRING: Hot buttered corn begs for the classic pairing for popcorn—champagne. Though not located within the Champagne region of France, Long Island produces some excellent sparkling wines. In fact, Sparkling Pointe in Southold is the only winery in New York State exclusively dedicated to the production of sparkling wines, and they're all created using the traditional *méthode champenoise*. For this dish, I suggest that you pour a flute of Sparkling Pointe Topaz Impérial Brut Rosé. Dry, yet a touch fruity and juicy, it's a great match for this corn.

Salt and Sugar Cured Fluke with Fresh Pickled Ginger

FOR THE PICKLED GINGER

1 tablespoon pink peppercorns

1 knob fresh ginger, about 2 fingers long

1¾ cups champagne vinegar

½ cup sugar

¼ teaspoon sea salt

¼ teaspoon ground cinnamon

FOR THE FLUKE

1½ cups kosher salt

½ cup sugar

3 organic lemon peels

2 fresh fluke fillets, skinless

¼ cup light brown sugar

½ cup peeled and grated raw red beets

1 teaspoon bottled horseradish with beets

Olive oil for drizzling

Small slices of bread for serving

1 lemon, quartered, for serving

Clean ginger trimmings, including skin, may be used to make a cup of ginger tisane.

You know the pink tinted slices of ginger that are served with sushi? Making them at home is quick and so much better tasting. I serve them with cured, paper thin slices of fluke (summer flounder) when it just comes to market.

Fluke is delicate and has a subtle fresh flavor, ideal for curing. It only takes 1 hour to cure the fish, and with this recipe, one fillet will be white, while the other will take on a beautiful dark pink color around the edges from being cured with beets. —*Hillary*

SERVES 4

1. To make the pickled ginger, put the pink peppercorns in a sealable plastic bag, close the bag, then smash them a couple of times with a rolling pin to coarsely crack them.

2. Peel the ginger with a vegetable peeler, then slice the ginger into thin slices with a small sharp knife.

3. In a medium saucepan, add the vinegar and ½ cup sugar and cook over medium heat until the sugar is dissolved. Add the sea salt, cinnamon, and the cracked pink peppercorns. Add the sliced ginger and cook it for about 4 minutes at a gentle simmer. Take off the heat, cool to room temperature, remove the ginger pieces to a bowl or jar, submerge with some of the cooking liquid, cover, and refrigerate until ready to use.

4. To prepare the fluke, put 1 cup of the kosher salt, ½ cup sugar, and lemon peels in the food processor and process until the peels are finely chopped. Put a large piece of parchment paper on a plate, scoop out the mixture from the food processor onto the parchment paper, add one of the fluke fillets and press down both sides into the mixture to thoroughly coat. Cover with the parchment paper, place on a plate, lay something heavy over the fish, and refrigerate for 1 hour.

5. In a glass or metal bowl, mix together ½ cup of the kosher salt, light brown sugar, the grated beets, and the horseradish, mashing them all together with a fork until well blended and the salt and sugar are stained pink. Lay a large piece of parchment paper on a large plate, scoop this mixture onto it, then lay the other fluke fillet on it and gently press the mixture onto both

sides to thoroughly coat. Wrap the fillet in the parchment paper, place on a plate, put something heavy on it to weigh it down, and refrigerate for 1 hour.

6. Rinse both the fillets under cold running water to remove the coating. Pat dry.

7. On a cutting board, using a sharp knife, slice the fillets against the grain into very thin slices.

8. Place a long piece of plastic wrap on the counter and put the fluke slices on it. Drizzle with a little olive oil, cover with another piece of plastic wrap, and, using a rolling pin, gently hit the fluke slices until they flatten into very thin slices.

9. To serve, alternate pink and white pieces of fluke on each plate, siding with small slices of bread, the pickled ginger, and a quartered lemon.

STACY'S PAIRING: The traditional partner for cured fish is ample shots of vodka. Long Island Spirits original LiV Vodka, made from Marcy potatoes, is a local favorite for its creamy mouthfeel and vanilla notes.

Long Island Potato Salad with Blue Cheese and Honey Vinaigrette

3 pounds small potatoes, boiled until just tender, cut into bite-size pieces

2 tablespoons honey

½ teaspoon freshly ground black pepper

¾ cup olive oil

¼ cup apple cider vinegar

½ teaspoon kosher salt

3 scallions (white and green parts), coarsely chopped, or ½ cup chopped kale stems

1 cup (4 ounces) crumbled blue cheese

¼ cup chopped cilantro

Cilantro or mustard flowers for garnish

Potatoes, cauliflower, and cabbage were huge commercial crops on Long Island's North Fork and South Fork through the late 20th century. Our rich, but sandy and well-drained soil is peerless for growing these crops and others. Commercial production continues, but in recent decades increasing real estate prices have sprouted many "house farms" across our fields.

I'm quite partial to sweet and sour in combination. My grandmother's German potato salad was my whole family's favorite dish. This salad is lightly dressed and beautiful when made with a selection of small potatoes in an array of hues. It can be served warm or cold.

To make cheesy home fries with leftover potato salad, simply drain all the liquid away and place the leftovers in a baking dish in which they fit snugly. Bake at 400°F for about 15 minutes, until golden brown on top. —Stacy

SERVES 6

1. Place the prepared potatoes in a serving bowl.

2. To make the vinaigrette, combine the honey and the pepper in a small saucepan. Allow the honey to infuse over very low heat for about 5 minutes. Turn off the heat, but leave the pan in place. Stir the oil, vinegar, and salt into the honey mixture in the saucepan. Stir in the scallions, cover and allow them to rest until fully wilted, about 5 minutes. Whisk the vinaigrette mixture and pour it over the potatoes. Just before serving, fold in the blue cheese and cilantro. Serve warm or at room temperature. Garnish with cilantro.

STACY'S PAIRING: The sweetness and complexity of this dish beg for a sparkling wine with a touch of complementary sweetness. Sparkling Pointe Brut provides it.

CILANTRO

Cilantro, perhaps more than any other fresh herb, sharply divides people into two camps: the lovers and the haters. This is largely because, for some people, its aldehydes taste similar to soap. Crushing the leaves diminishes this taste sensation, but you'll want to check with your dinner guests before using cilantro in a dish. Fresh flat-leaf parsley may be substituted for fresh cilantro in their servings.

Cilantro turns brown when cooked, dingy brown. So, to keep the flavor but avoid a murky appearance when cooking with cilantro in a dish, such as a soup, bundle a bunch of cilantro stems together with cotton string and remove the bundle before serving.

I'm an unabashed cilantro lover, and, happily, so are my family members. For me, it's not just cilantro's flavor that I love. I adore that cilantro is the first herb that comes up from seed in the spring—I plant it every fall. Its bright green leaves are a refreshing sight—a promise of more good things to come. Cilantro's life cycle is a brief one; it goes to seed very quickly. I plant more of it again in the spring and early summer.

Cilantro's seeds, when dried, are called coriander. This has caused confusion over the years—before many Americans knew cilantro well, cilantro was called "green coriander." Nowadays green coriander refers to fresh, still-green cilantro seeds. It is a favorite ingredient among chefs, and for good reason. These seeds are potent flavor bombs, like cilantro on steroids, and they can really spice up a dish. I recommend using them sparingly, applying them late in the preparation of slow-cooked meat dishes. —*Stacy*

Wedge of Watermelon Topped with Arugula Salad

FOR THE SALAD

1½-inch-thick wheel of watermelon

6 generous handfuls arugula, washed and dried

4 ounces Parmigiano-Reggiano

FOR THE VINAIGRETTE

6 tablespoons extra virgin olive oil

2 tablespoons cider or sherry vinegar

1 teaspoon Dijon mustard

½ small shallot, minced

¼ teaspoon sea salt

2 tablespoons finely chopped herbs (I use chives and tarragon)

For me, the presentation of a dish is as important as the flavor. I arrange this minimalist salad of greens and pink on a big white round serving plate, with lots of empty white around it.

Alternatively, I serve it individually, waiting at everyone's place setting before they arrive at the table. In that case, I choose overly large white plates and totally cover a wedge of the watermelon with the salad, so it is a surprise found underneath.

Using the ripest watermelon you can find, and the most tender young leaves of arugula, demonstrates that there is nothing better than simple food, prepared well. —*Hillary*

SERVES 4

1. Slice the wheel of watermelon into quarters and place one quarter on the center of each plate.

2. Put arugula into a mixing bowl. Make the vinaigrette by whisking together the olive oil, vinegar, mustard, shallot, salt, and herbs. Pour the vinaigrette over the arugula and massage it into the greens with your hands. Divide the dressed arugula over the watermelon wedges, mounding it high and covering the watermelon underneath.

3. With a vegetable peeler or small sharp knife, shave the Parmigiano-Reggiano over the top and serve.

STACY'S PAIRING: This blend of sweet and savory cries out for a well-balanced, sweet-tart Riesling like Martha Clara Vineyards Estate Reserve Riesling.

Nightshades and Farro Salad, a.k.a. "Hamptonata"

FOR THE FARRO

1 cup farro

1 bottle or can of ale (optional), such as Montauk Brewing Company Summer Ale

1 tablespoon extra virgin olive oil

¼ teaspoon kosher salt

FOR THE HAMPTONATA

¾ cup olive oil

1 pint Padrón peppers (about 5 ounces) or other mild pepper, destemmed and cut into bite-size chunks

1 large yellow onion, chopped

1 large eggplant or zucchini, cut into bite-size pieces

1 large boiling potato, cut into bite-size pieces

2 garlic cloves, smashed

½ cup red wine vinegar

1 teaspoon kosher salt

¼ teaspoon freshly ground black pepper

3 large tomatoes

10 fresh basil leaves, plus more for garnish

My family once had architect Fulvio Massi over for dinner. All of our dinners are potlucks. I don't remember what Fulvio and his wife Naimy Hackett brought, but my husband made caponata because we thought it'd be a good fit.

Fulvio said, "Caponata! I've always wanted to try that."

I said, "But you're from Italy."

And he said, "Yes, but not that part of Italy."

We agreed that his tasting caponata for the first time in America was pretty hilarious, but it also made a good point. The best food is local, and regional recipes evolve around that fact.

I've always enjoyed caponata but not the chunks of stiff celery in it. And the need for imported ingredients like capers and olives never grabbed me. So, here's my local take on the classic, "Hamptonata."

You could take the time to remove the tomato skins, if you'd like to, but I like the texture they add. I do peel away any skin that happens to come loose when I'm cutting the fruit into chunks. —*Stacy*

SERVES 6

1. There's no need to soak the farro ahead of cooking. Just place it in a medium saucepan with the 4 cups cold water (or 2½ cups water plus the bottle of ale, if using) and boil until softened but chewy, about 30 to 35 minutes. I like to use the light ale for a flavor boost.

2. Stir in the extra virgin olive oil and ¼ teaspoon kosher salt and set the farro mixture aside until you're ready to use it.

3. To prepare the Hamptonata, heat the ¾ cup olive oil in a large frying pan over high heat.

4. Cook the peppers, onion, eggplant, potato, and garlic in the oil for 10 minutes, stirring occasionally. Stir the vinegar, 1 teaspoon kosher salt, and black pepper into the mixture. Reduce the heat to low; cover and simmer until the potatoes are fork tender, about 10 minutes.

5. Core the tomatoes and cut them in half crosswise. Push out most of the seeds with your fingers. Coarsely chop the tomatoes. Stir the tomato chunks into the vegetable mixture. Cook the mixture over high heat until boiling. Remove it from the heat and stir in the basil. Allow the Hamptonata to rest at least 5 minutes before serving. This dish may be served warm or at room temperature—just be sure that the farro and the vegetables are close in temperature.

6. To serve, drain the farro and strew it onto the plates, then use a slotted spoon to portion vegetables onto the center of each plate. Garnish with the fresh basil leaves.

STACY'S PAIRING: Easy, laidback ales like Montauk Brewing Company Summer Ale or Driftwood Ale work well with this cooked tomato dish.

BLT Macaroni Salad with Ham Crisps

FOR THE DRESSING

1 cup sour cream

1 cup mayonnaise

3 slices bacon, cooked crisp and crumbled

2 tablespoons white balsamic vinegar

1 teaspoon Dijon mustard

½ teaspoon sea salt

2 teaspoons minced garlic

2 teaspoons sugar

Dash hot sauce

FOR THE SALAD

8 ounces elbow macaroni

2 tablespoons olive oil

4 ounces prosciutto

7 medium tomatoes, diced (reserve the juice)

½ iceberg lettuce, finely chopped

16 ounces thick-cut bacon, cooked crisp and crumbled

One of the most vivid pleasures of any summer is that first taste of a perfectly ripe tomato. Sometimes I find mine for sale at a table set at the end of a nearby driveway, where, if I get up early enough, I find tomatoes with dew still clinging to them, smelling of earth and morning.

Two of my indulgences for lunch in the summer are a bowl of macaroni salad or a BLT sandwich. So, tomatoes are on my mind from the moment I wake up.

Once I score the sweetest tomatoes I can, I return home knowing my day is made. It's either going into be a fabulous BLT or a macaroni salad. One greedy day I combined the two, not willing to give up one for the other. This was the result. Super easy. Super fun. Super delicious, if you have the best tomatoes ever. —*Hillary*

SERVES 4 TO 6

1. Put all the dressing ingredients into a food processor and process until well blended. The bacon will disintegrate and add a boost of flavor to the dressing. Cover and chill for at least 2 hours to allow the flavors to combine.

2. Cook the macaroni according to package instructions, drain into a sieve, then run under cold water to stop the cooking and help cool the pasta. Drain again.

3. Pour the olive oil into a frying pan and heat until shimmering hot. Add the prosciutto and cook until crisp and shriveled, 30 to 45 seconds. Drain on a paper towel.

4. When ready to make the salad, pour the pasta into a large bowl, cover it with the dressing, and toss well to thoroughly coat. If the dressing is not liquid enough, this is the time to use the reserved tomato juice to thin it. Fold in the tomatoes, lettuce, and crumbled bacon.

5. Arrange the prosciutto crisps across the top of the salad, and serve.

STACY'S PAIRING: Relax with a light, well-balanced ale. Montauk Brewing Company Driftwood Ale, an English pale ale, is so easygoing it welcomes this rich mix of creaminess, garlic, bacon, and tomatoes to the seaside party.

Muskmelon Ball Salad with Midori Vinaigrette

When I lived in France, we were enamored with the amazing little Cavaillon melons when they came to market. Now that I live in the Hamptons, I am finding the same enthusiasm and anticipation for the arrival of our epic muskmelons. Juicy and super sweet, they taste almost identical to the Cavaillon melons.

When muskmelons are in season I make sure to buy one every day. I slice and enjoy them in the morning, and I also use them to make this easy-to-prepare salad with a melon-flavored liqueur vinaigrette, which lights up the coral color of the melon with a vibrant green.

Because muskmelons vary in size, it's hard to predict how many balls a given melon will yield. Buy one and ball it so there is enough for four servings. Save the rest for breakfast. —Hillary

1 large muskmelon, balled
3 tablespoons extra virgin olive oil
6 tablespoons Midori liqueur
½ teaspoon sea salt

SERVES 4

1. Divide the melon balls between 4 small bowls.

2. Whisk together the oil, Midori, and sea salt. Pour over the melon balls and serve.

Not-Your-Average Burger with Beer Cheese

FOR THE BEER CHEESE

3 tablespoons unsalted butter

3 tablespoons flour

½ cup pale ale, more if needed

2 teaspoons Dijon mustard

1 teaspoon white wine Worcestershire sauce

¼ cup heavy whipping cream

8 ounces sharp Cheddar, grated on the big holes of a box grater

Dash of cayenne pepper

At a dinner the night before the annual Hamptons Classic Horse Show in Bridgehampton, I found myself seated at a formal table adorned with bone china and Baccarat crystal flutes filled with champagne. We were offered a choice of a luscious loin of pork with a balsamic and rosemary sauce, or what was presented to us on a mirrored silver platter: a pyramid of burgers piled precariously high. Guess what most of us chose.

I amused myself with the thought that, wherever you were in the Hamptons on that very hot summer night, burgers were sure to appear, either on a silver platter or straight off a backyard grill. And this was the impetus for this recipe. I wanted to serve them off the grill, but make them a bit more interesting, not-your-average burger.

I latched onto the idea of creating a thick Welsh rarebit topping. Traditionally made with strong Cheddar and ale, I thought it would be delicious and fun. I found my Cheddar at Mecox Bay Dairy, called Farmhouse Cheddar. It is aged and creamy and has enough spunk to stand up to a hamburger. And it's good enough for a silver platter. —*Hillary*

SERVES 4

1. To make the beer cheese sauce, melt the butter in a medium saucepan over medium-low heat. Add the flour and whisk for 2 minutes. Add the beer, mustard, and Worcestershire sauce and whisk to combine. Add the cream, whisk, then simmer until the sauce thickens. Add the cheese and cayenne pepper and stir vigorously until melted and smooth. You want the beer sauce to be thick and hold its own shape on top of the burger. However, if you think it looks too thick, add a bit more beer and whisk. Keep warm until ready to serve.

2. For the burgers, put the ground chuck, mayonnaise, egg yolk, salt, and pepper, to taste, into a large bowl and mix with your hands until well combined. Form the burger patties with your hands, taking care not to compact them too tightly, and grill over high heat, or broil, to desired doneness.

3. Slice the buns. Put a burger on each bottom bun, ladle over the beer cheese, add a slice of tomato, add the lettuce, cover with the top bun, and enjoy.

STACY'S PAIRING: An easygoing ale like Montauk Brewing Company Driftwood Ale is an easy match, but consider also the grape. Channing Daughters Winery Mudd Red Table Wine, with its savory blending of Merlot, Syrah, Dornfelder, Cabernet Franc, and Blaufränkisch, plays nicely with cheesy dishes like this one.

FOR THE BURGERS

2 pounds ground chuck

2 tablespoons mayonnaise

1 large egg yolk, lightly whisked

1 teaspoon sea salt

Freshly ground black pepper to taste

4 burger or potato rolls or large brioche buns

4 thick slices ripe tomato

4 leaves frilly lettuce

The egg white may be refrigerated in a sealed container for up to 4 days for another use.

Grilled Breaded Swordfish Steaks with Piccata Sauce

FOR THE SAUCE
Zest of ½ organic lemon
Juice of 1 organic lemon
¼ cup extra virgin olive oil
¼ cup heavy whipping cream
4 tablespoons (½ stick) unsalted butter
2 tablespoons minced fresh flat-leaf parsley
2 tablespoons small capers in brine

FOR THE SWORDFISH
4 swordfish steaks, 1 inch thick, at room temperature
2 organic lemons: 1 halved and 1 quartered for garnish
Sea salt and freshly ground black pepper to taste
4 heaping tablespoons mayonnaise
½ cup Italian seasoned bread crumbs
½ cup Panko bread crumbs
½ teaspoon sea salt
2 tablespoons minced fresh flat-leaf parsley

Swordfish are caught mid-June through September off Montauk. It's a big game fish, able to race through the sea at a thrilling 50 miles an hour. This tremendous fish is a prize for any fisherman and yields thick sturdy steaks.

I read that in Sicily they often bread swordfish before grilling, so I played around with the technique and found it eminently suitable to honor such a noble fish. The swordfish steaks become crispy on the outside and are kept juicy on the inside by the layer of mayonnaise. —*Hillary*

SERVES 4

1. Preheat the grill to medium-high.

2. Add the sauce ingredients to a small saucepan and heat until the butter is melted. Keep warm.

3. Rub the swordfish steaks with the lemon halves. Generously sprinkle with salt and pepper on both sides of the fish. Smear each swordfish steak all over with the mayonnaise.

4. Whisk the two kinds of bread crumbs, ½ teaspoon salt, and parsley together in a shallow bowl. Lay each swordfish steak in the bowl one at a time, turning over to coat them in the bread crumbs, and gently press down so the bread crumbs adhere.

5. Grill until just done, about 4 to 7 minutes on each side, using two forks to turn them over rather than a spatula, which could pull off the bread crumbs. Depending on how thick the steaks are, you will want to cook them until the bread crumbs are golden and the fish is just cooked. Try not to overcook them.

6. To serve, place one swordfish steak on each plate and divide the sauce equally, spooning it around the steaks.

STACY'S PAIRING: Look for a light beer with a touch of fruity sweetness to counter the lemon and capers on this substantial fish. Great South Bay Brewery Blonde Ambition Blonde Ale is just that—a mild Belgian-style ale with fruit.

Fishermen's Soup with Fresh Tomatoes and Basil Oil

Filled with layers of seafood, this is a soup you eat with both a spoon and a fork.

It is similar to a French bouillabaisse, but it is easier to make. For this rendition, I break with tradition and use chicken stock to cook the fish in—many tries with fish stock produced a less than stellar flavor. I also like the way the flavors come together with the mussel and clam broth.

The soup is finally anointed with a glistening of fresh basil oil, blessing it with impressive flavor before it comes to the table. —*Hillary*

SERVES 6

1. Make the basil oil by first putting ice in a medium bowl of cold water. Bring a small saucepan of water to a boil, add 1 tablespoon of the sea salt, and drop in the basil leaves to blanch them for 10 seconds. Blanching the fresh leaves of herbs like basil preserves their striking green color. Scoop them out and drop them into the ice water. Remove the leaves to paper towels and pat dry. Drop the leaves into a blender or food processor, add the ¾ cup olive oil and ½ teaspoon of the salt, and process until smooth. Pour the basil mixture into a jar with a lid. Reserve.

2. To make the soup, scrub the mussels and clams under cold water. Throw away any that do not close when you tap them on the counter, or any that are damaged.

3. Pour the wine into a large saucepan and heat over medium heat. Put the mussels and clams in, cover, and cook in stages: starting with the smallest, taking them out with a slotted spoon when opened, removing them to a plate, then putting in the next biggest. When they open, take them out and finish with the largest. This way they all cook properly and the broth achieves layers of shellfish flavor. Discard any that do not open.

4. Pour the broth into a bowl covered with cheesecloth, or a paper towel, so that you strain off any sand, and reserve the broth. Put the mussels and clams into a large bowl.

5. In a large soup pot, heat the 3 tablespoons olive oil, add the shallot, and cook over medium heat until they are golden.

Continued . . .

FOR THE BASIL OIL

1 tablespoon plus ½ teaspoon sea salt

1 cup fresh basil leaves, packed

¾ cup extra virgin olive oil

FOR THE SOUP

1 pound mussels

12 cherrystone or littleneck clams

2 cups white wine

3 tablespoons extra virgin olive oil

1 large shallot, diced

6 sun-dried tomato halves packed in oil

4 garlic cloves, finely chopped

½ teaspoon sea salt

32 ounces chicken stock

1 pound firm white fish such as cod or halibut

1 pound shrimp

7 tomatoes on the vine

½ cup grated Pecorino Romano

3 scallions, sliced thinly for garnish

Sliced baguette for serving

6. Finely chop the sun-dried tomatoes. Add them and any oil they had with them into the pot. Add the garlic and cook a further 3 minutes. Pour in the reserved mussel-clam broth. Add in the ½ teaspoon salt and stir.

7. In another medium soup pot, or deep frying pan, add the chicken stock and bring to a simmer. First poach the white fish until just cooked, timing depending on the thickness and size of your fish, making sure not to over-cook it. Remove the fish from the broth and reserve. In the same stock, cook the shrimp until just cooked, about 2 minutes, so that when you slice into one of them it is barely opaque in the center. Remove from the stock and reserve.

8. Pour the chicken stock into the pot of mussel-clam broth.

9. Finely dice the fresh tomatoes; do not peel or seed them. Add the freshly chopped tomatoes with their juices to the soup. Whisk in the grated cheese until it melts.

10. Pour all of the broth into a large serving bowl. Gently layer the fish, then the clams and mussels and shrimp, into the broth. Garnish with the scallions, drizzle with the basil oil, and serve with sliced baguette to dip into the soup.

STACY'S PAIRING: White wine is traditional for fish, but a light rosé like Wölffer Estate Vineyard Summer in a Bottle Rosé works well with the acidity of the tomatoes in this dish.

Peach Rosemary Glazed Grilled Chicken and Peaches

8 chicken thighs, skin on

1 tablespoon extra virgin olive oil, plus more to coat chicken

Sea salt and freshly ground black pepper to season

1 cup peach preserves

2 teaspoons Dijon mustard

2 teaspoons Balsamic Vinegar Glaze (recipe follows) or store-bought balsamic glaze

1 large garlic clove, crushed in a garlic press

½ teaspoon sea salt

2 teaspoons finely chopped rosemary leaves

2 ripe peaches, cut in half and pitted

The extra balsamic glaze may be stored in a covered jar in the refrigerator for up to three weeks. It can be drizzled on salads, pastas, and sandwich fillings.

We usually dine outdoors every summer night, when each puff of air brings with it the smell of the grills cooking in backyards on either side of us. Hamptons specialties emerge from these backyard grills and wood-burning pizza ovens. It's a bit of Americana illustrated with a flag out front and hot dogs and hamburgers out back.

In every historic village, from Westhampton to Montauk, residents are patriotically turning out roasted corn and steak, whole fish, lobsters, clams, burgers, hot dogs, and chicken.

For your own mouth-watering grilling feast, start with ripe peaches. When you grill ripe peaches, the interiors sweeten and will almost melt in your mouth. Serve them with grilled chicken that you have smeared with peach preserves and fresh rosemary, for two rounds of peachy goodness. —*Hillary*

SERVES 4

1. Rub the chicken thighs with olive oil to coat them all over and generously season with the salt and pepper.

2. Make the peach glaze by putting the peach preserves in a bowl, adding the 1 tablespoon olive oil, mustard, balsamic glaze, garlic, ½ teaspoon sea salt, and rosemary leaves, and whisking well to combine.

3. Preheat the grill to high. Place the chicken thighs on the grill skin side down and cook until beautifully golden, about 12 to 15 minutes. Timing will depend on how thick the thighs are, so test once they look the way you want them to.

4. Brush the thighs with the peach glaze (reserving some for the peaches) and cook about 5 minutes more, glazing and turning over at least twice until they look luscious. Remove to a platter to rest.

5. Place the peach halves on the grill cut side down and cook for about 3 minutes, or until they have developed grill marks. Turn them over, and brush with the peach glaze. Cook this way for a couple of minutes, then turn them over again to the cut side to cook until they look and feel done, according to your taste.

6. Serve the chicken and peaches with any extra peach glaze in a bowl to the side.

Pour the balsamic vinegar into a small, nonreactive frying pan. Stir in the honey. Heat just to the boil over medium heat. Reduce heat to low, add the port, and simmer until reduced by about half, stirring occasionally, until reduced by half. The glaze should coat the back of a spoon.

Balsamic Vinegar Glaze

1 cup balsamic vinegar
¼ cup honey
3 tablespoons port

STACY'S PAIRING: Look for a light, only slightly sweet white wine to pair with the over-the-top sweet and herbaceous elements of this dish. A Viognier could work well; Jamesport Vineyards Sauvignon Blanc definitely does.

Grilled Heirloom Tomato and Ricotta Pesto Pizza

In the summer, row after row of fresh herbs appear at outdoor markets, beside bunches of sunny gold and olive green sunflowers and tomatoes so plump you just want to squeeze them. Can you imagine how easy it is to throw together dinner with such a suggestive tableau?

Arriving with a main dish in mind, then eagerly accepting whatever seasonal bounty is presented on stands such as this (and ditching my original main dish for the opportunity to improvise with whatever is on offer) is the epitome of joyful cooking for me.

There's nothing easier than putting what I find on top of a pizza that's grilled outdoors. Those same finds can go into a salad served with it. Sunflowers in a tall vase. Lanterns lit. Beer and wine chilled. Heaven.

Pizza dough is a breeze to make, or you can buy a disk of fresh dough from your nearest and dearest pizza parlor. Here's my recipe for pizza dough. You pick your toppings at your favorite local stand. —*Hillary*

SERVES 4

1. To make the dough: Place 1¼ cups warm water in a small bowl. Sprinkle the sugar and the yeast over the water. Stir with a fork to combine. Set the mixture to rest and bubble for 8 minutes.

2. Place the flour, ½ teaspoon salt, oil, and crushed garlic in the work bowl of a food processor fitted with a dough blade or a standing mixer fitted with a dough hook. With the machine running on low, slowly pour in the yeast mixture. Process until a ball forms and then for an additional 30 seconds.

3. Turn the dough out onto a lightly floured board. It may be sticky. Knead the dough a few times, until smooth, adding a bit of flour, if necessary.

4. Lightly oil a large mixing bowl. Add the dough ball to the bowl and then turn it over to coat it. Cover the bowl with a damp towel and leave in a warm place to rise until it doubles in volume, about 45 minutes.

5. To make the ricotta pesto, place the basil leaves, 1 clove sliced garlic, pumpkin seeds, ½ teaspoon of the sea salt, vinegar, 3 tablespoons olive oil, and both cheeses in the clean work bowl of a food processor fitted with a

Continued . . .

FOR THE PIZZA DOUGH

1 teaspoon sugar

1 package (2¼ teaspoons) active dry yeast

3⅓ cups flour, plus more if needed

½ teaspoon fine sea salt

¼ cup olive oil, more for bowl and grill

2 garlic cloves, crushed in a garlic press

FOR THE TOPPING

2 cups fresh basil leaves, plus more for garnish

1 garlic clove, sliced

½ cup pumpkin seeds

1½ teaspoons sea salt

1 tablespoon white balsamic vinegar

3 tablespoons olive oil, plus more to drizzle

½ cup Pecorino Romano, freshly grated

1 cup ricotta

2 large heirloom tomatoes

Sea salt and freshly ground black pepper to taste

chopping blade. Process until smooth and spreadable. Add a bit of olive oil if needed to thin it.

6. Slice the tomatoes into thin slices. Drizzle them with olive oil, sea salt, and pepper.

7. Turn the dough back out onto the floured board and punch it down. Let it rest for 5 minutes, then roll it out into a rough rectangle, about ½ inch thick.

8. Preheat the grill to medium-high. Lightly oil the grill with olive oil, place the rolled-out dough on it, and grill until it has started to stiffen and grill marks have begun to show, for 2 to 3 minutes. Turn the crust over and cook for about 2 minutes. Pull it to the cool side of the grill to rest.

9. Brush the crust with olive oil and spread on the ricotta pesto, leaving about ½ inch bare around the edges. Arrange the tomatoes slices atop the pesto.

10. Close the grill and cook for another 2 to 3 minutes, or until the bottom is a crispy brown. If the dough is browning but the toppings still need more time, lower the heat and let cook for an additional 2 minutes.

STACY'S PAIRING: Champagne is a classic companion to salty, cheesy pizza. Indulge North Fork-style with local sparkler Sparkling Pointe Brut Séduction.

Roasted Black Sea Bass with Japanese Eggplant

Black sea bass are caught off Montauk from June to December. It's so easy to roast them whole, because they take only minutes to cook. I always roast them with olive oil, sea salt, slices of lemon and tomato, and a dose of crushed pink peppercorns. I pair them with delicate roasted Japanese eggplants, because you can cook them both in the same oven in almost the same amount of time.

You can find Japanese eggplant in our farmers' markets. They are light purple and long and thin, and less bitter than big black eggplant. The skin is thinner, so there's no need to peel it, and it roasts beautifully. It makes a lovely light side dish for the fish, which you can also serve with rice. Any roasting pan juices make a great drizzle for the rice. If you would like to pair the flavors of the eggplant with the fish, when roasting the fish eliminate the lemons and tomatoes and instead brush it liberally with the same sauce you use to roast the Japanese eggplant.

Always check the eyes of fish you buy. They should be clear and moist and plump and slightly protruding, not sunken or flat or cloudy. The flesh of the fish should bounce back to the touch and be firm. And fish shouldn't be smelly, but rather should smell fresh or have no smell at all. Ask the fish person when the catch came in. You want fresh fish, not fish that is two days old. —*Hillary*

SERVES 4

1. Ask your fishmonger to scale, gut, and rinse the fish for you so they are ready to bake. Ideally, you want to cook them the same day you buy them.

2. Put the peppercorns in a sealed plastic bag and hit them vigorously with a rolling pin until you crush them, or crush them in a mortar and pestle. Reserve.

3. Preheat the oven to 450°F. Line a roasting pan with parchment paper and lightly oil.

4. Lay the fish in the prepared pan. Salt and pepper the inside of their bellies, then stuff them with some of the slices of lemon and the dill.

Continued . . .

FOR THE FISH
Two 2-pound whole black
   sea bass
3 tablespoons whole pink
   peppercorns
Olive oil for roasting pan
   and to coat fish
Sea salt to season and scatter
4 lemons: 3 sliced thinly,
   1 quartered for garnish
½ bunch dill, fronds only
4 ripe tomatoes, thinly sliced

FOR THE EGGPLANT
4 Japanese eggplant
¼ cup mirin
2 tablespoons teriyaki sauce

5. Rub or brush oil all over the fish. Lay the remaining lemon slices and the tomato slices around the fish. Scatter sea salt and the peppercorns over the top.

6. Cut the stem caps off the eggplants, slice the eggplants vertically, and line up the slices on a rimmed baking sheet. Whisk the mirin and teriyaki sauce together then brush the mixture over the top of the eggplant slices.

7. Place the sheet of eggplants and the roasting pan with the fish in the oven to bake. Take the eggplant out in about 15 minutes, when it is soft. Take out the fish in 20 to 25 minutes, when they reach an internal temperature of 145°F, or flake easily. The time will vary due to size and weight of fish, so it's best to check with an instant-read thermometer. You can also easily test the doneness of the fish with a toothpick stuck into the center. If it is hard to pull out, the fish is not done yet. If it comes out easily and cleanly, the fish is done.

8. To serve, you can bring the fish to the table on a large platter and carve them there, or carve them in the kitchen and serve individual portions on plates.

9. To carve each fish, begin by using a small knife to pull away the fin bones on the edges of the fish and remove them. Then move up the fish to the head, and slice down at the intersection of the head and the collarbone. Then move to the bottom of the fish, and slice down to separate where the tail meets the fish flesh. Slice the fish horizontally along the spine that separates the back of the fish from the bottom (belly) of the fish. Once you find this location, gently slice down all the way along the fish and push away the top long piece of fillet onto the platter or cutting board. Next, slip the bottom belly fillet off the bones onto the platter or cutting board.

10. You can now see the spine, which you will lift from one end to the other and remove completely from the fish, pulling away any stray bones you see. Pull away the tail and the head to be left with just a fillet, and clean away any bones.

11. You will be left with long fillets, which you can arrange attractively on a serving platter, or slice up and serve individually. Side with the roasted Japanese eggplant and a wedge of lemon.

STACY'S PAIRING: This dish calls for a beer with some gravitas and marginal bitterness. Long Ireland Beer Company Celtic Ale is a traditional Irish ale that can take on this rich mix of eggplant, teriyaki, dill, and delish fish with ease.

Just-Picked Peaches and Whipped Cream Angel Food Cake

FOR THE CAKE

12 large egg whites without a speck of yolk in them, at room temperature

¼ teaspoon fine sea salt

½ teaspoon almond extract

2 teaspoons pure vanilla extract

1½ teaspoons cream of tartar

1½ cups superfine sugar

1 cup cake flour

FOR THE TOPPING

1 pound fresh ripe peaches, skin on, sliced

2 tablespoons sugar

3 tablespoons Wölffer Estate Vineyard Descencia dessert wine or Grand Marnier

FOR THE WHIPPED CREAM

1 cup heavy whipping cream, chilled

2 tablespoons superfine sugar

1 ounce Wölffer Estate Vineyard Descencia or Grand Marnier

I spied a woman walking out of a store with a wooden fruit box full of peaches. As I passed her, the peach perfume followed and haunted me as I entered the store. My thoughts became laser focused on making something with what were obviously juicy, just-picked peaches.

And as memory has a way of popping up at just the right time with a matching vision, I saw the towering angel food cake I used to make years ago. Inspiration struck. I would slice up fresh peaches and fill the center of the cake, then mound with heaps of Grand Mariner–spiked whipped cream.

Here is a memory come to life, as good this time as it was then. Remember, it's all about the peaches. —Hillary

SERVES 8 TO 10

1. Preheat the oven to 325°F. Line the bottom of a 10-inch two-piece tube angel food cake pan (very dry and ungreased) with parchment paper.

2. In the bowl of a stand mixer, add the egg whites, salt, almond and vanilla extracts and beat until the mixture becomes frothy. Add the cream of tartar and slowly beat in the 1½ cups superfine sugar until the mixture is glossy and forming soft peaks. Do not beat until stiff.

3. Remove the bowl from the stand mixer and sift the flour over the top. Very gently fold in the flour, trying not to lose volume or overmix. Scoop into the baking pan, put it in the oven, and bake for 45 to 55 minutes, until golden brown. It will be done when a cake tester comes out clean and it springs back when touched.

4. Remove the cake from the oven and allow it to stay in the baking pan for 1½ hours. Insert a knife around the edges, cover the cake pan with a board, invert the pan and the board, and while holding with both hands, hit the pan on the board so the cake comes out of the pan.

5. Toss the peaches in the sugar and dessert wine, and refrigerate them while the cake is cooling.

6. To make the whipped cream, beat the whipping cream with the 2 tablespoons superfine sugar until the cream holds soft peaks. Beat in the dessert wine, cover, and refrigerate until ready to use.

7. Present on a beautiful cake stand or large plate with a bowl of the whipped cream and a bowl of the peaches. Alternatively, you can pile the peaches into the center well of the angel food cake, mound with heaps of whipped cream, then serve. Gently slice into servings with a serrated knife so as not to deflate it.

Egg yolks may be refrigerated in a sealed container for another use within 4 days.

STACY'S PAIRING: Wölffer Estate Vineyard Descencia, made from late harvest Riesling and Chardonnay grapes, is lush with the flavor of golden raisin, hinting at apricot. This dessert wine, with its lively concentration of sweetness and fruit flavor, is naturally superb paired with this peachy confection. Or, for something more "devilishly" good, try a sip of Montauk Rumrunners Honey Flavored Whiskey. Just a sip . . .

Blueberry Madonna Pie

The first time I picked wild blueberries, I hiked a long way up a small mountain near my mother's house in southern New Hampshire to find them. It was the beginning of blueberry season, and cars were already parked along the dirt road leading to a trail curling upward through the pine-scented woods.

I met an Indian woman at the top. Her purple and gold sari fluttered in the wind and her enormous smile radiated joy like the golden rays that radiate from a Madonna's halo. She said she loved to come up here to pick blueberries and enjoy the mountain air. She waved me on to take my turn at the bushes. I turned to ask what she was going to do with them. "Make blueberry curd, of course!"

As soon as I got home, after a long five-hour drive, I picked through the berries, gently cleaned them, and found a recipe to make blueberry curd, which I then turned into a pie, and which I continue to make every summer here in the Hamptons. I named the pie Blueberry Madonna Pie, after the woman who was my inspiration. —Hillary

SERVES 8

1. Add the flour, salt, and confectioners' sugar to a food processor and pulse six times. Distribute the ½ pound butter over the top and pulse until it forms a coarse meal.

2. Add the vanilla to 4 to 6 tablespoons ice water, then turn on the machine and drizzle in the water just until the dough begins to come together. Scoop the dough onto a floured clean work surface. Use your hands to bring it together into a ball. Flatten it into a disk, cover it, and chill for 2 hours.

3. Roll out the dough to a 12-inch circle and place it in a 10-inch pie plate. Turn over the edges to make a thicker crust and put it in the refrigerator to rest for 20 minutes.

4. Preheat the oven to 400°F.

5. Prick the bottom of the dough with a fork a few times, cover with parchment paper, weigh down with pie weights or dried beans, and bake 10 minutes.

Continued . . .

FOR THE CRUST
2½ cups flour
½ teaspoon fine sea salt
2 tablespoons confectioners' sugar
½ pound (2 sticks) unsalted butter, cold and cut into pieces
1 teaspoon pure vanilla extract

FOR THE SYRUP
3 cups fresh blueberries
½ cup sugar

FOR THE FILLING
½ cup sugar
⅓ cup cornstarch
4 large egg yolks
1 teaspoon pure vanilla extract
1 to 2 tablespoons fresh lemon juice
2 tablespoons unsalted butter, in small pieces
¼ cup blueberry jelly or jam
Fresh mixed berries to decorate top of pie

The egg whites may be refrigerated in a sealed container for up to 4 days for another use.

6. To make the blueberry syrup, bring 1 cup water, blueberries, and ½ cup sugar to a boil in a medium saucepan, stirring as it comes to a boil. Reduce the heat and simmer for 10 minutes. Allow the berry mixture to cool to room temperature and then whiz in a blender until smooth. Reserve.

7. Preheat the oven to 325°F.

8. To make the filling, whisk together the ½ cup sugar and cornstarch in a small bowl.

9. Pour 2 cups of the blueberry syrup into a medium saucepan. Add the cornstarch and sugar mixture and whisk well to combine. Whisk in the egg yolks until combined. Over medium-low heat, bring to a simmer then whisk or stir until the mixture becomes very thick, about 8 to 10 minutes. Whisk in the vanilla and 1 tablespoon lemon juice. Taste and, if desired, add another tablespoon of lemon juice. Add the 2 tablespoons butter and whisk until melted and well blended.

10. Pour the blueberry filling into the piecrust and bake for 15 to 20 minutes, until firm around the edges but still a little wobbly in the center. Cool the pie to room temperature. Melt the blueberry jelly in a small saucepan on the stove and brush it over the top of the pie so that it glistens. Decorate with fresh mixed berries and serve.

STACY'S PAIRING: A glass full of Duck Walk Vineyards Blueberry Port is just the thing to complement the multilayered flavors of this blueberry treat. The blueberries used to make this popular port are not locally grown; it benefits greatly from the intense flavor of Maine blueberries.

Miracle Crust Peach-Berry Pie

This is the pie that seduced the self-described "insatiable" food critic Gael Greene. I interviewed her to promote a reading she was giving. When I went to the event, I took along a big basket containing homemade pie and jars of preserves. I'd read all about her and I'd read many of her restaurant reviews and novels, but I didn't know that Gael had a long-standing tradition of eating pie for breakfast while staying in the Hamptons. The next day she thanked me for the pie in an e-mail, referring to it as "very rustic." I wasn't sure if that was good or bad until she tweeted to the world that it was "the best!" We've been friends ever since.

If, by some odd circumstance, you have a slice of peach pie left over after a few days, you can drop it into the blender when you're making a batch of vanilla milkshakes for a special treat. —Stacy

SERVES 8

1 batch Miracle Piecrust (see page 142)
6 medium yellow peaches, peeled and sliced
1 cup packed light brown sugar
¼ cup cornstarch
2 tablespoons white wine vinegar
½ teaspoon cinnamon
½ teaspoon freshly grated nutmeg
½ pint (about 6 ounces) blackberries

1. Prepare the Miracle Piecrust on page 142. Place it in a 10-inch pie plate.

2. Preheat the oven to 425°F.

3. Place the peaches, sugar, cornstarch, vinegar, cinnamon, and nutmeg in a medium mixing bowl and gently stir to combine them. Fold the blackberries into the peach mixture.

4. Pour the filling into the crust. Cut a 2-inch circle out of the center of the top crust to vent steam. Cover the pie with the top crust. Use a fork to crimp the edges together by pressing it down along the rim of the pie plate, trimming off any excess crust.

5. This pie will likely drip when it's baking, so wrap the pan loosely with a solid sheet of heavy duty aluminum foil to catch any spills. Bake the pie about 50 minutes, until the crust is golden brown. Allow the pie to cool for at least 1 hour before serving. Cutting it while it's still hot will make the filling appear watery.

STACY'S PAIRING: A light, not-too-sweet rosé like Wölffer Estate Vineyard Summer in a Bottle Rosé fits the bill here. It melds with the dish, much like the pronounced sweetness of the sugared peaches is countered by the acidity of the berries.

Miracle Piecrust

1 tablespoon bacon fat, chilled

1 cup less 1 tablespoon vegetable shortening

8 tablespoons (1 stick) unsalted butter, plus more for the pie plate

2¾ cups all-purpose flour, plus more for the pie plate and work surface

¼ cup whole wheat flour

1 egg

1 tablespoon apple cider vinegar

My great-great grandmother Rosa Weinke passed this piecrust recipe down. It was a common one back in the day. Farm wives could not afford to have a cake fall or a piecrust not be flakey, and they used what they had at hand to make them work every time.

Grandma Weinke and her neighbors favored using Crisco as soon as it came out in 1911. It was considered a labor-saving improvement over rendering pig fat. And I can testify to the fact that cooking down a pig for lard does not smell pretty. Crisco was also handy because it did not require refrigeration. In tweaking her recipe, I added a bit of "the pig" back in for flavor. If you choose to cut out the bacon fat, replace it with a tablespoon of butter and ⅛ teaspoon fine sea salt. You can replace the shortening in this recipe with clarified butter; the crust will just not be quite as resilient.

Leftover crust can be rolled out, fitted into a small baking dish, and wrapped and frozen for future use. It lasts about a month in the freezer. Just let frozen crusts rest at room temperature for about an hour before you use them—they don't have to thaw out completely. Do not refrigerate this dough, as that could make it tough.

To make piecrust cookies, cut out desired cookie shapes, sprinkle them with cinnamon sugar, and bake them in a 400°F oven for about 15 minutes, until golden brown. —*Stacy*

MAKES ENOUGH CRUST FOR A TWO-CRUST PIE PLUS DECORATIVE ADDITIONS

1. Place the bacon fat in a one-cup measure and then fill the cup with shortening to total 1 cup.

2. Place the shortening mixture and butter in a medium mixing bowl and mix both flours in with a potato masher until the dough is a mass of lumps.

3. Place the egg in a cup and beat it slightly with a fork. Add 5 tablespoons cold water and the vinegar to the cup and mix with the fork.

4. Incorporate the egg mixture into the flour mixture with a potato masher, adding it about a third at a time.

5. Butter and flour a 10-inch pie plate.

6. Roll out the crust to an 11-inch circle of ¼-inch thick dough. Use a large spatula to loosen the circle of dough from the work surface. Then use the spatula to fold the dough in half, then into quarters. Place the dough in the pie plate and unfold it. Follow this rolling and lifting process again to form a top crust, if needed.

7. Press the bottom dough with your fingertips to line the pie plate, allowing a generous ½-inch to cover the rim. If you are making a two-crust pie, you can cut out any shapes you like with the extra dough and attach them to the top crust by wetting the back side of each of them with water and placing them.

Flourless Espresso Chocolate Hazelnut Cookies

2 teaspoons Medaglia d'Oro Instant Espresso Coffee

⅔ cup unsweetened dark cocoa powder

1 teaspoon ground cinnamon

½ cup dark brown sugar

¼ teaspoon fine sea salt

¼ teaspoon baking powder

1 cup bittersweet chocolate chips

3 large eggs, at room temperature, separated

⅔ cup sugar

2 teaspoons pure vanilla extract

1½ cups plus 2 tablespoons confectioners' sugar

1 cup finely chopped hazelnuts

On a night when the sun set spectacularly with streaks of gold and pink, I headed to a Labor Day clambake on the beach. As the evening progressed, the party overflowed down to the edge of the surf for dancing barefoot in the sand to a DJ spinning reggae. We were saying goodbye to a warm dreamy summer spent near the ocean.

Although the event was catered, it was essentially a simple clambake serving clams, lobsters, and corn, and lots of melted butter, so the guests were encouraged to bring something additional to our last feast. I brought a really big platter of these cookies.

Earlier in the day I had passed a sign by the side of the road proclaiming "fresh local eggs," swung in the driveway, enthusiastically bought too many of the multi-hued eggs, and decided to use them to bake my flourless chocolate cookies.

Fantastic, veritable flavor bombs of espresso and chocolate, they have personalities strong enough to stand up to any Vino Santo or brandy. Which is how I served them to my friends that night, with a tray of shots of Vino Santo to dunk them into. —Hillary

MAKES ABOUT 2 DOZEN COOKIES

1. Into a small bowl, add the instant espresso, cocoa powder, cinnamon, brown sugar, salt, and baking powder. Whisk to combine.

2. Melt the chocolate chips in a small saucepan over low heat. Cool to room temperature.

3. In the bowl of an electric mixer, beat the egg whites until they form stiff peaks.

4. In another bowl, beat the egg yolks with the sugar until pale. Add the vanilla and beat to combine.

5. Add 1 cup and 2 tablespoons of the confectioners' sugar to the egg yolks and use a spoon to combine. Add in the espresso-cocoa mixture. Mix in the melted chocolate and hazelnuts. The dough will be hard to work.

Continued . . .

6. With a spoon, mix in one-third of the beaten egg whites to combine. Spoon in the next one-third and mix. Fold in the final third. The mixture will be thick.

7. Preheat the oven to 375°F. Line two baking sheets with parchment paper.

8. Let the dough sit for 20 minutes to harden a bit. This will make it easier to handle, although it will still be sticky to work with. Dust your hands with confectioners' sugar before you hand roll the cookies to make it easier to work the dough.

9. Sift the remaining ½ cup confectioners' sugar onto a large piece of parchment paper.

10. Scoop 1 rounded tablespoon of the dough at a time into the palm of your hand, roll into a ball, drop it onto the confectioners' sugar on the parchment paper and roll around to gently coat. Shake off any excess sugar, and place 2 inches apart on the prepared cookie

11. Bake 9 to 10 minutes, until tops crack. The cookies will be very soft. Remove the cookies from the oven, allow them to cool for 10 minutes on the baking sheet, then transfer to a plate.

STACY'S PAIRING: A pure Petit Verdot wine like Channing Daughters Winery Petit Verdot is the rare red that is deep and dark enough to match chocolate note for note. On the other local hand, there's a powerful match to be had with Greenport Harbor Brewing Company Golden Stout. This beer itself is made with precise additions of coffee and chocolate.

Chapter Four

FALL

Labor Day to Thanksgiving

In the fall, as the tree leaves turn brilliant colors
and the corn stalks rustle in the wind, every edible plant
that has not yet fruited comes into season. It's time to
celebrate pumpkin-apple-pear-raspberry-squash
season with an autumnal feast!

SMALL PLATES

Blackened Brussels Sprouts and Sunchokes   151

Cod Mashed Potato Mini-Cakes   152

Caramelized Sweet Potato Slices   154

Savory Mushroom Bread Pudding   156

Roasted Montauk Pearl Oysters   158

SALADS

Quick-Pickled Pumpkin Salad with Candied Pumpkin Seeds   160

Green Salad with Roasted Cinnamon Bosc Pears   163

Crispy Shredded Potato Pancake with Warm Pink Applesauce   164

Arugula, Goat Cheese, Cranberry Salad with Salt and Pepper Popovers   166

MAINS

So Many Tomatoes Sauce over Spaghetti Squash   168

Wild About Striped Bass   170

Eggplant "Farm" Lasagna   171

Fondue-Filled Baked Acorn Squash with Chunks of Country Bread   174

Heritage Turkey Breast   176

Confit Turkey Legs and Wings   178

Turkey Splits   179

DESSERTS

Long Island Cheese Pumpkin Pie   180

Flourless Chocolate Cake with Raspberry Cabernet Consommé   182

Farmhouse Apple Pie   184

Fall Fruit Granola Crumble   186

East End Cheeseboard   188

Blackened Brussels Sprouts and Sunchokes

I first had blackened Brussels sprouts as a small plate at a hip restaurant in Portland, Maine. Served alongside cold beer, they're a great starter.

You can also use this recipe with cauliflower or broccoli florets and chopped stems, but with one added step: Mix the salt and pepper with the olive oil before pouring the oil over the floret mixture. Otherwise, the salt and pepper could clump and reach only a few pieces of the cauliflower or broccoli.

You can shred the Brussels sprouts and sunchokes in a food processor for a delish "hash." Just "slice" the cooking times in half. —Stacy

SERVES 6

1. Preheat the oven to 425°F. Line a rimmed baking sheet with parchment paper.

2. Cut very large sprouts in half and large chokes into bite-size pieces. Place the vegetables in a large mixing bowl and drizzle them with the olive oil, then sprinkle with the salt and pepper. Stir to coat. Spread the vegetables over the baking sheet so that they are not touching each other. Bake for 12 minutes. Turn the baking sheet around in the oven and stir the vegetables with a spatula for even baking. You don't want any loose leaves on the baking sheet throughout the cooking process because they will turn to ash—so be sure to remove any loose leaves and enjoy them! Bake for another 12 minutes.

3. Remove the baking sheet from the oven and group the vegetables together on it. Drizzle the butternut squash seed oil over them and spread the vegetables out again. Bake the vegetables about 5 minutes more, until they are quite dark.

4. Place the vegetables in a serving bowl and drizzle with the leftover oil from the baking sheet. Serve hot or warm.

1 quart (about 1¼ pounds) Brussels sprouts
1 pint (about ½ pound) sunchokes, unpeeled
⅓ cup olive oil
1 teaspoon kosher salt
1 teaspoon freshly ground black pepper
2 tablespoons butternut squash seed oil or pumpkin oil

STACY'S PAIRING: These blackened morsels are a great starter when served on toothpicks with a very cold, medium-bodied India pale ale like Oyster Bay Brewing Company IPA.

Cod Mashed Potato Mini-Cakes

Everybody loves garlic mashed potatoes, and flaked cod adds richness to the mashed potato experience. We recommend using organic Yukon Gold potatoes because many conventionally farmed Yukon Gold potatoes have been genetically modified to produce toxins within the tuber itself to kill pests. Also, most conventionally farmed potatoes today are coated with chlorpropham or maleic hydrazide to prevent sprouting. Organic potatoes are not treated with these growth inhibitors. As always, it pays to know your farmer. If you use conventional potatoes for any dish, we recommend that you peel them. —Stacy

MAKES 30 MINI-CAKES

1. Preheat the oven to 400°F. Line two baking sheets with parchment paper.

2. Place the cod in a shallow baking dish and generously salt and pepper the fillet. Bake the cod for 10 minutes. Remove the cod from the oven and allow it to cool. Drain the cod and use your hands to break the fish into flakes.

3. Place 1 teaspoon of the kosher salt in a large saucepan and fill the pot about halfway with cold water. Place the saucepan next to a cutting board. Quarter the potatoes and place them in the pot as you work, so they don't discolor.

4. Boil the potatoes 15 to 20 minutes, until they are soft. Drain off the water, leaving the potatoes in the pot. Add the butter to the potatoes and mash them. Stir the cod, cream, and garlic into the potato mixture. Season with salt and pepper.

5. To make the coating, mix the bread crumbs, dill, and remaining 1 teaspoon kosher salt together in a shallow dish, such as a pie plate.

6. Form the potato mixture into balls of about 2 tablespoons each with your hands. Roll the balls in the bread crumb mixture to coat. Place the balls on the prepared baking sheets and flatten slightly with your hand.

7. Bake for 10 minutes, turn the baking sheets around and bake about 10 minutes more, until the mini-cakes are thoroughly heated. Garnish with paprika (if using) and serve hot or warm.

STACY'S PAIRING: Fish, garlic, dill, and creaminess beg for a simple white wine like a pure Sauvignon Blanc. Locally, I quite like Channing Daughters Winery Sauvignon Blanc.

1 pound cod fillet

2 teaspoons kosher salt, plus more for the fillet

Freshly ground black pepper to taste

2 pounds organic Yukon Gold potatoes, peeled

2 tablespoons unsalted butter

2 tablespoons heavy whipping cream

6 garlic cloves, crushed in a garlic press

2 cups fine, dried bread crumbs

2 teaspoons dried dill or chives

Paprika (optional)

Leftover mini-cakes can be briefly fried in hot oil until a little crispy for a treat.

Caramelized Sweet Potato Slices

½ small yellow onion

3 tablespoons maple syrup

3 tablespoons grapeseed or olive oil

½ teaspoon freshly ground black pepper

⅛ teaspoon red pepper flakes

¼ teaspoon sea salt

3 pounds (about 4 large) sweet potatoes (or 2 medium acorn squash, scrubbed, seeded and coarsely chopped)

Chives, freshly snipped, for garnish (optional)

I used to enjoy a marshmallow-topped sweet potato dish as much as the next kid, but nowadays I prefer to walk that sweet/savory line. Every year I look forward to Sagaponack farmer Marilee Foster's fall crop of golden sweet potatoes, which taste like candy. I like to accent them with onion essence. While I wait for Marilee's taters, any colorful orange variety of sweet potato works just fine. —Stacy

SERVES 8

1. Preheat the oven to 425°F. Line two baking sheets with parchment paper.

2. Place the onion, maple syrup, oil, black pepper, pepper flakes, and sea salt in the work bowl of a food processor and process until a fine, wet mixture forms.

3. Peel the sweet potatoes. Cut the potatoes lengthwise and then into half-circles about ½-inch thick. Place the slices into a medium mixing bowl. Pour the onion mixture over the potato slices and stir to coat.

4. Place the potato slices on the prepared baking sheets so that they're not touching each other. Bake for 20 minutes. (This dish can be prepared ahead to this point and set aside until you wish to finish cooking it.) Turn the potato slices over, and bake them about 10 to 15 minutes more, until they are golden brown.

5. To serve, place in a serving bowl and garnish with the chives.

STACY'S PAIRING: A light India pale ale with a hint of sweetness like Montauk Brewing Company Session IPA works well with this dish. Alternatively, a spicy and very balanced rosé like Palmer Vineyards Merlot Rosé could also enhance the enjoyment of this dish.

Savory Mushroom Bread Pudding

5 tablespoons unsalted butter

4 garlic cloves, minced

1 large baguette (26 inches), stale

2 tablespoons olive oil

1 small yellow onion, minced

1 medium leek, chopped

1 medium shallot, minced

8 ounces mild mushrooms such as baby bella or button, thickly sliced

2 ounces shiitake mushroom caps, thickly sliced

1 teaspoon fine sea salt, plus more for sprinkling

½ teaspoon dried lovage or celery seed

½ teaspoon ground white pepper

1 teaspoon freshly ground black pepper

1 teaspoon dried sage

1 cup whole milk

¼ cup chicken or vegetable stock

2 large eggs

Of course this dish is "savory"; sweet mushrooms are not a popular thing. I included the word in this recipe title to stress how very savory it is—a rich combination of umami (mushrooms), butter, alliums, and salt meets with some caramelization in neat servings. I enjoy the custardy aspects of a traditional dressing as much as I like the crunchy bits—so I developed this dish to maximize both.

Many recipes advise removing bread crusts before making bread into bread crumbs. But I often prefer to include crusts in order to increase the overall caramelization in the dish.

Cooks have long been advised not to rinse mushrooms but to simply brush them free of debris in order to avoid sogginess. I grew up on a farm, so I know where mushrooms have been. I always rinse mushrooms and quickly pat them dry with a soft kitchen towel. I can't tell you how many times I've been served gritty mushrooms in restaurants, but it's close to the number of times I've sent them back. —*Stacy*

SERVES 8

1. While the oven is preheating to 400°F, place 4 tablespoons butter in a 9-by-13-inch baking dish and put it in the oven for a couple minutes to melt. Remove the dish from the oven. Stir the garlic into the melted butter in the pan. Spread the garlic around the pan.

2. Cut the heels from the baguette and reserve them. Cut the remaining loaf into 16 pieces.

3. Arrange the 16 pieces of bread snugly in the baking dish. Bake for 5 minutes. Remove the pan from the oven and turn the pieces of bread over. Bake for 5 minutes more and then remove the pan from the oven. Leave the oven on.

4. Heat the olive oil and the remaining 1 tablespoon of butter in a medium frying pan over medium heat. Place the onion, leek, and shallot in the frying pan and sauté them until they are translucent and tender, about 5 minutes. Add all of the mushrooms, salt, lovage, both peppers, and sage to the frying pan and sauté over medium-low heat until tender and somewhat reduced, about 5 minutes.

5. Place the milk and stock in a large measuring cup. Lightly beat the eggs into the milk mixture with a fork.

6. Spoon the mushroom mixture over the baking dish full of bread. Pour the milk mixture over all. (This dish may be prepared to this point and refrigerated, covered, for baking later. Just let it rest at room temperature for an hour before placing it in the oven and give it 5 to 10 additional minutes of baking time.) Bake the pudding, uncovered, about 20 minutes, until it is golden brown.

7. While the pudding bakes, grate the heels of reserved bread on the large holes of a box grater or in a food processor.

8. Remove the pudding from the oven and sprinkle it with the bread crumbs and sea salt. Bake for about 5 minutes more, until the crumb topping is very crispy.

STACY'S PAIRING: White bread soaked in mushroomness cries out for a white wine with earthy notes. McCall North Ridge Vineyard Sauvignon Blanc Cuvée Nicola delivers on that and offers a hint of wildflowers.

Roasted Montauk Pearl Oysters

2 dozen Montauk Pearl oysters (or other variety)
½ pound (2 sticks) unsalted butter
1 shallot, minced
1 tablespoon white wine
2 teaspoons red wine vinegar
Fine sea salt to taste

My father-in-law once told me a story about his being so poor that, when he was a runner on Wall Street, he would take shortcuts through bars to score a free meal. In those days in Lower Manhattan, oysters were so plentiful that they were considered poor man's food. Bars would serve platters upon platters of freshly shucked oysters. If he bought a beer, my father-in-law told me, he could eat all the oysters he could manage. This story pointedly reminds me of how abundant they once were, and what they are today—a scarce luxury to be treasured.

They used to be bountiful here in the Hamptons, and it is just one reason why we are making a concerted effort to encourage local oyster farming.

I treasure each and every luscious one. Most of the time I tip their shells toward my lips and slip them down raw with a mignonette sauce, but for company I roast them in the following way. —*Hillary*

SERVES 4

1. Scrub the oysters well under cold running water and do not dry as the moisture will help to open them in the oven. Discard any open oysters and any with broken shells.

2. Preheat the oven to 425°F. Put a pan of water in the bottom of the oven as it heats up, and leave it there while the oysters roast. It will make it easier for them to open.

3. In a frying pan, melt the butter, add the shallot, wine, and vinegar and stir to combine. Take off the heat and add salt to taste.

4. Put the oysters on a rimmed baking sheet, place in the oven, and as each one pops open, take it out of the oven. It should take from 6 to 9 minutes. Throw away any oysters that do not open.

5. Hold each oyster in an oven mitt and use a dull knife to fully open each one. Divide the oysters between four plates, drizzle sauce onto them, and serve immediately.

STACY'S PAIRING: *Que Syrah?* Because a Syrah like Martha Clara Vineyards Syrah works with this shellfish dish. It has both the backbone and body to support the vinegar and shallot, and its acidity provides a pleasant contrast to the heart of the matter, the buttery oyster flesh.

HAMPTONS OYSTERS

Here on Long Island, oysters were once plentiful and cheap; that is no longer true. However, there is a concerted effort to increase yield, and local oyster farming is growing. Floating oyster farms can be found in Noyac Bay, Peconic Bay, Gardiner's Bay, off Montauk, and more are planned. East Hampton Town is encouraging oyster farming by offering licenses to town residents who would like to try growing their own.

Like wine, oysters have a terroir—called *merroir* because it is marine rather than earthen (terra)—each one looking and tasting different depending upon where they are harvested.

For instance, Mecox Bay oysters are wild, harvested from the deep bay where they grow at the bottom almost 30 feet down. They have a mild, crisp flavor. They are allowed to be harvested and purchased from mid-November through the end of April. Because of this limited season, they are in high demand.

Farmed oysters to enjoy include Peconic Golds, Peconic Pearls, Montauk Pearls, and Shinnecock "Chief" oysters. The Shinnecock "Chief" oysters are farmed by the Shinnecock Indian Nation in Southampton. The Indians farm their oysters from the muddy bottom of the bay (as opposed to in floating surface trays), producing really large mature oysters.

Montauk Pearls are grown in floating trays in Napeague Bay off Montauk. They reap the rewards of being near the ocean, and they are ultra-clean, fat, salty, and slightly sweet. They have deep cups and a polished shell.

Peconic Pearls have medium cups and are salty and savory. Peconic Golds have quite deep cups and are full of flavor. Both are from Peconic Bay. —*Hillary*

Quick-Pickled Pumpkin Salad with Candied Pumpkin Seeds

FOR THE SALAD

1 tablespoon honey

2 teaspoons bottled horse-radish

2 teaspoons kosher salt

1½ teaspoons fresh ginger, peeled and grated on a microplane

½ teaspoon dried chile flakes

½ pound chunk of raw pumpkin or butternut squash

1 large bunch (about 14 ounces) curly kale, coarsely chopped, stems removed

FOR THE CANDIED PUMPKIN SEEDS

1 cup raw pumpkin seeds, or from a cooked pumpkin, shelled or unshelled

2 tablespoons olive oil

2 tablespoons honey

½ teaspoon kosher salt

¼ teaspoon ground white pepper

Pumpkin oil for drizzling

Clean ginger trimmings may be used to make a tisane.

I first enjoyed a pickled pumpkin salad at The Maidstone restaurant in East Hampton a few years back. It was so good, I got right to work on my own version. Mine is rather spicy hot, and you may wish to reduce the amount of red chile flakes.

This recipe makes more candied pumpkin seeds than you'll need for the salads, because the cook deserves a treat. —Stacy

SERVES 4

1. Combine the 1 tablespoon honey, horseradish, 2 teaspoons salt, ginger, and chile flakes in a medium mixing bowl. Stir together.

2. Using a vegetable peeler, skin the piece of pumpkin. Then use the peeler to cut the pumpkin into ribbons over the bowl containing the horseradish mixture, so the ribbons fall into it. Gently toss the pumpkin ribbons well to coat them. Cover the pumpkin with a large piece of parchment paper and weight it down so the paper is right on top of the pumpkin mixture. (A plastic bag full of about a pound of pasta, or another dried foodstuff, works well as a weight.) Let the mixture rest for about 30 minutes.

3. Preheat the oven to 300°F. Line a baking sheet with parchment paper.

4. To prepare the pumpkin seeds, place them in a small mixing bowl. Add the oil, 2 tablespoons honey, ½ teaspoon salt, and white pepper and stir to coat. Drain any excess liquid from the seeds. Spread the seeds out on the prepared baking sheet. If using seeds in the shell, bake for 20 minutes. Then flip the seeds over with a large spatula and continue to bake for about 15 minutes more, until golden brown. (If using seeds without shells, bake for 10 minutes, then flip the seeds over with a large spatula and continue to bake them for about 10 minutes more, until golden brown.)

5. Place the kale in a large mixing bowl. Add the pickled pumpkin and its liquid to the kale and use your hands to thoroughly mix the salad.

6. Divide the kale mixture among 4 salad bowls. Drizzle the salads with the pumpkin oil. Sprinkle the salads with the prepared pumpkin seeds and serve right away.

STACY'S PAIRING: The touch of horseradish in this dish corrupts the flavor experience of wine, so try a bright India pale ale like Long Ireland Beer Company West Coast IPA with its edge of hoppy bite.

Green Salad with Roasted Cinnamon Bosc Pears

Thank you to my friend Hilda Longinotti for the inspiration of doing a "dry rub" of cinnamon on pears before roasting them. I couldn't believe it would work on dry pears, but it does. The result makes a great addition to a fall salad. The pears' natural honeyed aroma intensifies as they bake, while the interior becomes sweeter and soft. —Hillary

SERVES 4

1. Preheat the oven to 325°F.

2. Wash and dry the pears. Slice each one vertically, so that you have 4 halves. Gently scoop out the core. You can leave on, or take off, the stem as you wish.

3. Sprinkle ½ teaspoon cinnamon on the cut side of each pear half and rub in. You want quite a thick coating of cinnamon on this side. On the skin side, dry rub on ½ teaspoon of cinnamon with your fingers. Place the pears on a rimmed baking sheet, cut side down (do not butter the baking sheet and do not line it with parchment paper).

4. Place in the oven and bake for 25 to 35 minutes, until fork tender. The timing will depend upon the size of the pears. I usually take mine out at 25 minutes, as they should not be mushy. Remove the pears and try to use them as soon as possible so that they are warm when you serve them.

5. While they are baking, make the salad by placing the salad greens in a mixing bowl.

6. Make the vinaigrette by whisking all the ingredients together in a small bowl.

7. When ready to serve, toss the salad with the vinaigrette and divide between 4 plates. Add one warm roasted pear, right out of the oven, to the side and serve.

FOR THE PEARS
2 Bosc pears, unpeeled
4 teaspoons ground cinnamon
Mixed salad greens, enough for 4 servings

FOR THE VINAIGRETTE
½ cup extra virgin olive oil
¼ cup sherry or apple cider vinegar
1 small shallot, minced
2 tablespoons honey, more if desired
2 teaspoons Dijon mustard

STACY'S PAIRING: You want a red wine with real body to stand up to the strong flavors in this vinaigrette—vinegar, mustard, shallot—and yet complement the spicy sweetness of the pears. For this I looked for a Cabernet Franc and Merlot blend, and I found it in Paumanok Vineyards Festival Red.

Crispy Shredded Potato Pancake with Warm Pink Applesauce

My mom's forays into our kitchen were rare, but when she cooked she gave it all her love. She wore an apron and very high heels, and there was a linear trail of notes along her kitchen counter.

Each note was a well-thought-out step toward her final creation. And each creation was beautiful, tasteful, and smart.

On this occasion, her last note read like the final sentence of a novel: "should be able to hear a harvest song from my apple picking."

This warm pink applesauce was one my mom made after harvesting red apples from our trees. When I make it, I can hear her song. —*Hillary*

SERVES 4 TO 6

1. Toss all the applesauce ingredients into a large saucepan with ½ cup water and bring to a boil. Reduce to a simmer and cook until the apples are soft and mushy, about 12 to 15 minutes. (The skins give the applesauce its beautiful pink color.)

2. Press this mixture through a fine metal sieve or food mill to remove the skins. Scoop the applesauce back into the saucepan, taste to see if you would like to add more sugar or spices, then cover and keep warm until ready to use.

3. Grate the potatoes on the big holes of a box grater. With both hands, gather up the potatoes and squeeze tightly over the sink to get rid of excess liquid. Toss them into a bowl. Sprinkle with the salt, pepper, cumin, and flour, then mix well with your hands or a mixing spoon.

4. Heat a large frying pan with the olive oil until very hot. Add the grated potatoes and pat down flat with a spatula into the shape of a pancake that fills the whole frying pan. Cover and cook over medium heat for 6 to 8 minutes, then check the bottom of the potato by gently lifting it up with a spatula around the edges. If it is beautifully browned and crisp, it is time to turn it over. If not, let it cook a minute or 2 longer.

5. To turn it over, place a plate large enough to cover the frying pan over the top and invert the potato pancake onto the plate. Then slip the potato pancake back into the hot frying pan to cook the other side until it is beautifully browned and crisp, about 3 minutes. Slip the pancake out of the frying pan onto a cutting board.

6. Slice the potato pancake into four equal pieces and place one piece in the center of each of four plates. Ladle some of the warm applesauce over half of each piece of pancake, scatter with the sliced scallions, and serve immediately.

STACY'S PAIRING: A light hard cider like Wölffer Estate Vineyard No. 139 Dry Rosé Cider is a good match for crispy-savoriness-meets-apple-sweetness.

FOR THE APPLESAUCE

1½ pounds any organic red apples, unpeeled, cored, cut into chunks

¼ cup light brown sugar, more if needed

2 tablespoons apple brandy or Calvados (optional)

2 teaspoons ground cinnamon, more if needed

½ teaspoon ground nutmeg, more if needed

FOR THE POTATO PANCAKE

2 medium russet potatoes, peeled

1 teaspoon sea salt

4 cracks freshly ground black pepper

½ teaspoon ground cumin

1 tablespoon flour

3 tablespoons olive oil

4 scallions, thinly sliced for garnish

Arugula, Goat Cheese, Cranberry Salad with Salt and Pepper Popovers

FOR THE POPOVERS

1 cup flour

1 teaspoon sea salt

4 cracks freshly ground black pepper

1 cup milk, at room temperature

1 tablespoon unsalted butter, melted

2 large eggs, at room temperature

FOR THE VINAIGRETTE

⅓ cup extra virgin olive oil

3 tablespoons white balsamic vinegar

1 tablespoon honey

1 tablespoon dried cranberries

1 teaspoon Dijon mustard

½ teaspoon sea salt

FOR THE SALAD

6 cups arugula

⅓ cup dried cranberries

3 ounces coarsely chopped hazelnuts

4 ounces goat cheese, crumbled

I serve a warm baguette and sweet butter to complement my salads, or sometimes I switch that out with flaky biscuits or quick popovers hot out of the oven. Lately I have been serving popovers more and more when I entertain since they are dead simple to make and keep their shape for a long time. I make the popovers ahead of time and toss the salad together in the last 15 minutes of the popovers' baking time.

Popovers hold a special place in my heart. I was introduced to them when my grandmother took us to a restaurant called Patricia Murphy, famous for their delicious hot popovers that "popover girls" would bring to your table in baskets.

Patricia Murphy built a restaurant empire based, I firmly believe, on her popovers. She was an amazing woman who by 1956 was serving over a million meals a year. My recipe is a slight variation on hers, taken from her book *Popovers and Candlelight,* and made every single time with Patricia in mind.

—Hillary

SERVES 4

1. Preheat the oven to 450°F.

2. Into a medium mixing bowl, sift the flour, salt, and pepper. Add the milk, butter, and eggs and, using an electric hand mixer, beat until the mixture is just smooth. Do not overbeat.

3. Generously butter the popover or muffin tin and fill each cup three-quarters full with the popover batter. Put the pan back in the oven and bake for 30 minutes. (Do not open the door.) Turn down the heat to 350°F and bake an additional 10 to 15 minutes, until the popovers are fully risen and golden brown and crusty.

4. To make the vinaigrette, put all the ingredients in a food processor and process 10 seconds.

5. Toss the arugula into a salad bowl, pour the vinaigrette over the top, and massage with your fingers until the leaves are entirely coated.

6. Add the cranberries and hazelnuts and toss to combine. Sprinkle the crumbled goat cheese over the top and serve with the warm popovers just out of the oven.

STACY'S PAIRING: A fully developed, but not heavy, Cabernet Franc like Kontokosta Winery Cabernet Franc Reserve fits the bill here. A year in Hungarian oak barrels lends a rich, savory underpinning, ideal for pairing with nuts and cheese.

So Many Tomatoes Sauce over Spaghetti Squash

5 pounds tomatoes, stem and blossom scars removed

2 large yellow onions, quartered

3 garlic cloves, smashed

1 teaspoon dried oregano

1 teaspoon freshly ground black pepper, plus more for the squash

¼ teaspoon red pepper flakes

1 teaspoon sea salt, plus more for the squash

1 cup olive oil, plus more for squash

1 large spaghetti squash for every 2 people you wish to serve

Fresh basil for garnish

Freshly grated Parmesan

Leftover sauce will keep covered in the refrigerator for up to 10 days, or frozen for up to 6 months.

We look forward to July 4th for the "fireworks" of the first local tomatoes. Now that the initial thrill is in the rearview mirror, remember that there's no such thing as "too many tomatoes." Here in the Hamptons we typically harvest tomatoes right up until Halloween. If you're full to bursting with fresh tomato sandwiches, bruschetta, and *salade tomates*, it's time to cook these local fruits down! This recipe will reduce 5 pounds of tomatoes to about 6 cups of delicious sauce. It takes a couple hours and yields luscious results. Though this sauce is best when you use local tomatoes, it works wonders with lesser tomatoes as well. Use one large spaghetti squash for every two people you wish to serve.

If you want to can some of this sauce, prepare to follow standard instructions for hot water bath canning, adding 1 tablespoon of vinegar to each pint jar of sauce, as soon as the sauce is ready. Do not allow the sauce to cool before canning. Visit the National Center for Home Food Preservation website for proper times and more information. —*Stacy*

SERVES 2 TO 8

1. Preheat the oven to 325°F.

2. Cut the tomatoes crosswise and use your fingers to remove most of the seeds. Place the tomatoes, onions, and garlic in one large baking dish (it's okay to really pack them in tight). Sprinkle all with the oregano, both peppers, and salt, and then drizzle with the oil. Roast for about 2 hours, until the vegetables are soft and starting to brown. Remove the dish from the oven and allow the vegetables to rest while you prepare the spaghetti squash.

3. Turn the oven up to 400°F.

4. Use a heavy, sharp knife to cut a bit of the stem end off each spaghetti squash to form a flat surface. Turn the squash onto its flat end and cut the squash in half lengthwise. Use a knife to cut around the seed cavity, and then scoop out the seeds with a spoon, leaving the thick fleshy walls intact. Rub about 2 teaspoons of olive oil over the inside of each squash half, including its cut surfaces, and sprinkle with salt and pepper. Place the squash on a second large baking dish cut side down and roast in the oven for about 45 minutes, until its shell is easily pierced with a fork.

5. Use a slotted spoon to remove the tomatoes and onions to a food processor. Puree the roasted vegetables until they reach the desired consistency. (I like to leave it quite chunky.)

6. Place the tomato puree and the olive oil left in the baking dish together in a saucepan and stir to combine. Keep the mixture warm for serving.

7. Just before serving, fluff the interiors of the squash with a fork to make the flesh more spaghetti-like.

8. Spoon about ¾ cup of the sauce into each spaghetti squash half and garnish with some fresh basil. Serve immediately with grated Parmesan on the side.

STACY'S PAIRING: The acidity of the tomatoes cries out for Chianti or perhaps a none-too-dry red like Pugliese Vineyards Sangiovese from the North Fork of Long Island. (Traditional Chianti is made with at least 80 percent Sangiovese grapes.)

Wild About Striped Bass

4 pounds fresh wild striped bass fillets of uniform thickness

4 tablespoons (½ stick) unsalted butter, melted

2 cups white wine (approximate), at room temperature

Sea salt and freshly ground black pepper to taste

Fresh thyme leaves (optional)

"Stripers" are by far the most popular fish to catch in Long Island waters. When Wölffer Estate Vineyard partner and winemaker Roman Roth told me that he liked them best oven-poached in Wölffer Estate Vineyard Perle Chardonnay, I had to try it. Roman is always right about food and wine.

I like to serve this fish with a whole-grain side dish. —*Stacy*

SERVES 8

1. Preheat the oven to 400°F.

2. Allow refrigerated fish to rest at room temperature for about 30 minutes.

3. Place the butter in a shallow roasting pan, rotating the pan to coat its bottom.

4. Arrange the fish in the roasting pan skin side down. Pour enough of the wine in the pan to come up to about half the thickness of the fish. Sprinkle fillets with salt and pepper and fresh thyme, if using.

5. Place the pan in the oven and cook until the fish is completely opaque, about 12 minutes per inch of thickness. Serve immediately. The pan juice may be strained and served as a jus with the fish and any whole-grain side dish.

STACY'S PAIRING: Like an identical rhyme, a dry white used in this dish, like Wölffer Estate Vineyard Perle Chardonnay, does work well with itself and this fish.

Eggplant "Farm" Lasagna

It seems cruel to have to choose between eggplant Parmesan and lasagna as a main dish, so I combined them. I call this "farm" because it uses so many locally grown ingredients in one dish. Feel free to replace the eggplant with zucchini or the carrots with some winter squash.

I started using tofu instead of ricotta (and doubling it to replace the mozzarella) in order to accommodate my vegan mother-in-law. I've found that I prefer the tofu to ricotta, but I missed the gooey mozzarella. Like so many tomato/vegetable dishes, this lasagna is even better reheated, so, if you can, make it a day ahead. —Stacy

SERVES 4 TO 6

1. Preheat the oven to 400°F. Line a large plate with paper towels.

2. Drain the tofu and place it in a medium mixing bowl. Mash the tofu with a fork and stir in the carrot, vinegar, salt, pepper, nutmeg, basil, oregano, and 2 tablespoons of the Parmigiano-Reggiano. (If using ricotta, omit the vinegar.)

3. Add just enough of the tomato sauce to coat the bottom of a 9-by-13-inch baking dish. Sprinkle the sauced pan with half the mushrooms. Place three lasagna noodles in the dish. Dollop the noodles with the tofu mixture and sprinkle with the remaining mushrooms. Place three more noodles in the dish. Place the sliced mozzarella over the noodles. Place three more lasagna noodles in the dish. Cover the lasagna with tomato sauce, reserving 1 cup of sauce.

4. Cover the dish with parchment paper and then cover it securely with heavy-duty aluminum foil and place it on a rimmed baking sheet to catch any spills. Bake for 1 hour. (This dish can be prepared ahead to this point. If you refrigerate it, allow it to come to room temperature before proceeding.)

5. Heat about 1 inch of oil in a frying pan to 350°F.

6. In a shallow bowl, beat the egg with a fork. Place 1 cup of the bread crumbs in another shallow bowl. Dip the eggplant slices in the beaten egg and then dredge them in the bread crumbs and add the slices to the hot oil. Fry the eggplant slices until they are golden brown on both sides, about 3 minutes per side. Place the fried eggplant slices on the paper towel–lined plate to drain.

Continued . . .

One 14-ounce package firm tofu or 15 ounces ricotta
1 medium carrot, grated
½ teaspoon apple cider vinegar
½ teaspoon kosher salt
½ teaspoon freshly ground black pepper
¼ teaspoon freshly grated nutmeg
½ teaspoon dried basil
½ teaspoon dried oregano
4 tablespoons freshly grated Parmigiano-Reggiano
1 quart tomato sauce
½ ounce dried mushrooms, such as porcini, crumbled
9 regular lasagna noodles
8 ounces mozzarella, sliced
Olive oil
1 large egg
2 cups Italian seasoned bread crumbs
1 medium eggplant, cut into ½-inch lengthwise slices

7. Mix the remaining cup of bread crumbs and the remaining 2 tablespoons Parmigiano-Reggiano together.

8. Pour the remaining 1 cup sauce over the top of the lasagna.

9. Arrange the prepared eggplant slices atop the lasagna, then sprinkle the bread crumb mixture all over the top. Bake, uncovered, in a 400°F oven for about 15 minutes, until the eggplant is tender. Allow to rest for a few minutes before serving.

STACY'S PAIRING: Choose a medium-bodied red wine with some flintiness like Bedell Cellars Merlot to give some foundation to the experience of the pepper and deep richness of the mushrooms and gooey cheese. There's just enough fruitiness in most Merlots, sometimes even a touch of berry, to counter the tomato, which plays a secondary role to the other vegetables in this lasagna.

Fondue-Filled Baked Acorn Squash with Chunks of Country Bread

2 acorn squash, washed and dried

2 medium garlic cloves, minced

1 cup white wine

¼ teaspoon freshly ground nutmeg

¼ teaspoon sea salt, plus more to taste

5 ounces white Cheddar, grated on large holes of a box grater

6 ounces Swiss cheese, grated on large holes of a box grater

2 tablespoons kirsch, brandy, or cognac

2 tablespoons cornstarch

Freshly ground black pepper to taste

Enough country-style bread for 4 people, cubed

After I come back home from happy hour at the old, red-brick American Hotel in Sag Harbor in the winter, where they offer fondue with drinks at the bar, I inevitably start obsessing about making fondue at home.

My yearning then leads me to locate interesting cheeses for my fondue, which I usually discover either at Cavaniola's Gourmet cheese shop in Sag Harbor or from the farm store at Mecox Bay Dairy, near my Bridgehampton home.

This fun appetizer is done in two steps: baking acorn squash in the oven and making the fondue on the stovetop. The acorn squash will hold the fondue, providing each guest with an individual serving.

Sometimes squash have shallow bowls, and to use all of the fondue you may need to keep your overflow of fondue warm on the stove to refill shells. The fondue recipe that fills them can be adjusted by adding more cheese or wine. —*Hillary*

SERVES 4

1. Preheat the oven to 350°F.

2. Cut each squash in half lengthwise. Then slice a small bit off the bottom of each squash half so that they sit flat. Use a spoon to scoop out the seeds and stringy bits.

3. Place the squash in a baking dish, cut side down. Pour ½ cup water into the baking dish and bake for 40 minutes. Turn over and cook another 10 minutes, if needed; otherwise, take out of the oven. The squash should still hold its shape, while the flesh is soft enough to eat.

4. The last 15 minutes the squash are baking you can begin to make the fondue.

5. In a large saucepan, add the garlic, wine, nutmeg, and ¼ teaspoon sea salt. Bring to a simmer. Add the cheeses and stir vigorously until melted. Add the kirsch and stir.

6. Put ¼ cup water and the cornstarch in a measuring cup and use a fork to combine them to mix a slurry. Add the slurry to the saucepan, stir over medium-high heat until the cheese smooths out and becomes thick.

7. Generously salt and pepper the insides of the squash. Pour the fondue into the shells. Serve immediately with cubes of bread to dunk into the fondue.

STACY'S PAIRING: Seek out a rather dry white wine that hints at fall fruit flavors like Paumanok Vineyards Chenin Blanc Dry Table Wine.

Heritage Turkey Breast

One 14-pound turkey, leg and wings removed (see confit recipe, follows)
3 cups poultry or vegetable stock
5 pounds root vegetables, cut into bite-size pieces (any combination of potatoes, carrots, celeriac, parsnips, turnips)
¼ cup duck fat
Fine sea salt and freshly ground black pepper to taste
Ground sage to taste
½ cup flour
2 cups white wine or water

Leftover gravy will keep covered in the refrigerator for 2 days.
Leftover meat will keep covered in the refrigerator for 3 to 4 days.

Heritage breed turkeys contain less fat than industry-adapted breeds, so it's not practical to roast the whole bird, as the dark meat in particular could end up tough.

Ask your farmer or butcher to cut the legs and wings free from the body. I confit the leg and wing pieces overnight and reheat them the following day to serve with the roasted breast fresh from the oven. Using these recipes, both the white and dark meats should be moist and flavorful.

It's helpful to use a roasting rack to keep the breast in place while it cooks, but large balls of heavy-duty aluminum foil can also be used on the two sides of the turkey to hold it in place.

This recipe is based on a 14-pound turkey. When you remove the neck, back, and organs for use in making stock, that leaves about 5 pounds of dark meat (legs and wings) and 6 pounds of bone-in breast meat. For a larger bird, you'll want to add about 15 minutes per pound of cooking time in both methods used below—confit and roasting. Altogether, this size bird feeds 10 and allows for leftover meat and gravy. Always bring gravy to a boil before serving it a second time. —Stacy

SERVES 10

1. Remove the turkey breast from the refrigerator to rest at room temperature for about 1 hour.

2. Preheat the oven to 425°F.

3. Pour 2 cups of the stock into 13-by-16-inch roasting pan. Add the vegetables to the pan in an even layer.

4. Pat the turkey breast dry. Rub the duck fat all over every surface of the breast.

5. Center the meat breast side up in the roasting pan. Sprinkle all generously with the salt, pepper, and sage. Place the pan in the oven to bake for 30 minutes.

6. Remove the pan from the oven just long enough to stir the vegetables around in the pan. Turn the pan around and place it back in the oven. Turn the oven down to 350°F and bake until the internal temperature of the turkey reads 165°F on an instant-read thermometer, about 1 hour. Turn the oven down to 200°F.

7. Remove the breast from the roasting pan to rest on a cutting board for at least 15 minutes before cutting to serve. Tent the resting meat with heavy-duty aluminum foil, lined with parchment paper, to retain heat and moisture.

8. Remove the vegetables from the baking pan with a slotted spoon and place them in a baking dish. Cover and place the dish in the oven to keep warm.

9. To make a gravy, place the roasting pan on a burner over medium-high heat and add the remaining 1 cup of stock. Use a wooden spoon to scrape the bits from the bottom and sides of the pan. Bring the contents to a boil, stirring occasionally. Meanwhile, stir the flour into the wine in a 4-cup measuring cup until no lumps remain. Slowly pour the wine mixture into the pan, while stirring. Bring to a boil and continue to boil, stirring occasionally, until thick and creamy, about 3 minutes. Turn the burner down to low and simmer for at least 5 minutes. Strain just before serving. Serve the gravy in a large gravy boat alongside the meat and vegetables.

To reuse the duck fat, scrape away all meat solids and juices, melt the fat, and strain it through cheesecloth. Pure duck fat will keep covered in the refrigerator for up to 3 months.

STACY'S PAIRING: An open, medium-bodied red like Anthony Nappa's Bordo Antico, a Cabernet Franc, that's just a touch spicy works well with this traditional bird and sides.

Confit Turkey Legs and Wings

2 turkey legs

2 turkey wings

8 cups rendered duck fat

½ cup kosher salt

2 bay leaves, broken into pieces

1 tablespoon dried marjoram

2 tablespoons dried parsley

1 teaspoon black peppercorns

½ teaspoon ground white pepper

Confitting was originally used to preserve meats and other comestibles. Many foods were stored "potted" (covered in fat) before the advent of modern canning techniques in the early 1800s. French chefs have preserved the tradition because it is so very tasty. —Stacy

SERVES 4

1. Remove the turkey pieces from the refrigerator and allow them to come to room temperature for about 1 hour.

2. Preheat the oven to 200°F.

3. Place the duck fat in a large saucepan to melt over lowest heat. Add the salt, bay leaves, marjoram, parsley, and both peppers to the melted fat and stir to combine. Leave over heat.

4. Pat the turkey pieces thoroughly dry. Place the pieces in a heavy ovenproof pot with a lid. Stir the melted fat to distribute the salt and herbs, then pour over the turkey pieces to cover. Cover the pot, place it in the oven, and cook for about 8 hours. Check doneness by carefully lifting a leg from the fat and piercing it with a paring knife. The meat should be extremely tender. Remove the pot from the oven and leave it uncovered to cool to room temperature. Once cooled, this pot can be covered and refrigerated overnight. (For longer storage it should be chilled so the meat juices congeal and can then be removed and the fat strained and re-applied before refrigeration.)

5. When ready to use, allow the confitted pieces of meat to come to room temperature if the pot has been refrigerated. Preheat the broiler to low (450°F). Gently remove the pieces from the fat and wipe away any excess fat. Place the pieces on a baking sheet and broil about 10 minutes, until nicely browned and heated through

STACY'S PAIRING: Confitted meat is very rich. You might choose to contrast it with a very dry white wine. The higher the alcohol content, the drier the wine. Look for a Sauvignon Blanc or Chardonnay above 11%. Locally, Bridge Lane Chardonnay fits the bill in more ways than one. As the more affordable division of Lieb Cellars, Bridge Lane wines are a great choice for serving a crowd. When it comes to the leftovers, especially when served as a Turkey Split (see opposite page), enjoy the more casual fare with a mild Belgian-style ale like Great South Bay Brewery Blonde Ambition Blonde Ale.

Turkey Splits

My husband, Dr. Daniel W. Koontz, is the proud inventor of the turkey split. Originally the idea was to use up holiday leftovers, but now it just seems like the way to live. —Stacy

SERVES 4

1. Mix horseradish with sour cream, if using.

2. Bring the gravy to a boil and then keep it warm over a low burner while you prepare the other ingredients. You may wish to add some soy sauce to make it darker, more chocolate-like, in color.

3. Reheat the turkey meat, both potato dishes, and the dressing.

4. In separate containers, mash the potato and the sweet potato dishes.

5. Place a bed of turkey in the bottom of each of four banana split dishes. Use an ice cream scoop to scoop one scoop of the white potatoes and one of the sweet potatoes over each bed of turkey. Form some of the dressing into rounded chunks similar in size to the scoops of potatoes and add them to each of the banana split dishes. Drizzle the three mounds in each dish with gravy. Dollop each center mound with the horseradish cream, if using. Garnish the center mound with two fresh sage leaves and a cranberry. Serve immediately.

STACY'S PAIRING: This casual leftover fare, in a rather formal presentation, is creamier and smoother than it was the first time it was served. Try enjoying it with a big spoon and a mild Belgian-style ale like Great South Bay Brewery Blonde Ambition Blonde Ale.

4 teaspoons bottled horse-radish (optional)
1 cup sour cream (optional)
2 cups turkey gravy (see page 176)
Soy sauce (optional)
2 pounds turkey meat, roasted or confitted (see pages 176 or 178)
2 cups mashed potatoes
2 cups mashed sweet potatoes
2 cups dressing or stuffing
Fresh sage leaves for garnish
Cooked cranberries for garnish

Long Island Cheese Pumpkin Pie

FOR THE CRUST

1 batch Miracle Piecrust (see page 142)

FOR THE FILLING

2 cups cooked pumpkin (see opposite page)

4 tablespoons (½ stick) unsalted butter, at room temperature

1 cup maple syrup or packed light-brown sugar

2 large eggs

2 tablespoons cornstarch

½ teaspoon ground cinnamon

½ teaspoon freshly grated nutmeg

¼ teaspoon ground ginger

½ teaspoon pure vanilla extract

Flour for rolling out dough

Whipped cream

The Long Island cheese pumpkin thrived in our soil and was popular through the 1800s in pies, soups, stews, pickles, and roasts. It kind of resembles a wheel of cheese in color and shape—it's a big, flat guy. And that was its downfall. Rounder, more brightly colored pumpkins inched it out until its seed was no longer sold in catalogs. Local seed saver Ken Ettlinger and the Long Island Regional Seed Consortium established the Long Island Cheese Pumpkin Project to "preserve and bring culinary awareness to this local variety." Their efforts have been very successful. No Long Island Thanksgiving table is now complete without this heirloom, though, in this dish, you can use the pulp of a sugar pumpkin or kuri squash. Any of these squash need to weigh at least 3 pounds to yield the required amount of pulp.

For how to make a decorative piecrust cookie, see directions for Miracle Piecrust on page 142. Allow the cookie to cool before placing it on the center of the pie.

Serve the pie warm or cold, with a dollop of whipped cream or ice cream—or both. —Stacy

SERVES 8

1. Prepare the Miracle Piecrust on page 142 through step 5.

2. Preheat the oven to 375°F.

3. Puree the cooked pumpkin in a food processor until smooth, about 20 seconds on high. Add the butter, maple syrup, eggs, cornstarch, cinnamon, nutmeg, ginger, and vanilla and puree together until smooth again, about 20 seconds on high, scraping down the sides of the work bowl as needed.

4. Coat a flat surface generously with flour and roll out the dough for one 10-inch crust. Place the crust in a 10-inch pie plate, pressing the dough with your fingertips to line the pie plate and to just stick up a bit above the inner edge of the pie plate. Fill it with the pumpkin mixture.

5. This pie will likely drip while it's baking, so wrap the pan loosely with a solid sheet of heavy-duty aluminum foil to catch any spills. Bake for about 1 hour, until the pie filling is firm. Allow the pie to cool for at least 15 minutes before serving. A few cracks are likely to form in the surface of the baked filling as it cools.

6. Serve pie warm or cold with a dollop of whipped cream.

Leftover pumpkin pulp can be frozen for use within a year.

The pumpkin seeds can be salted and toasted at 325°F for about 30 minutes, until they're golden brown, for use as a snack food. Since the seeds' shells have effectively been boiled, you should be able to eat them whole.

STACY'S PAIRING: Macari Vineyards Block E White Dessert Wine offers a complexity of flavors after its initial burst of sweetness, which suits this rich pumpkin dessert.

HOW TO COOK A PUMPKIN OR WINTER SQUASH

1. Preheat the oven to 400°F.

2. Remove the pumpkin's stem by knocking it against the edge of a countertop. Rinse and scrub the pumpkin's skin to remove any soil. Put the pumpkin in a large baking dish and add about 1 inch of boiling water to the dish. Place the dish in the oven and bake until the pumpkin's pulp is found to be tender when poked with a fork. This could take 45 minutes to 1 hour, depending on the size and density of the pumpkin. Remove the pumpkin from its cooking water to cool. When the pumpkin has cooled enough to handle, cut it in half and use a spoon to scoop out all of its seeds. Scrape or cut the pumpkin pulp from the rind.

—Stacy

Flourless Chocolate Cake with Raspberry Cabernet Consommé

FOR THE GANACHE

¾ cup Wölffer Estate Vineyard Cabernet Franc or other Cabernet Franc

¾ cup heavy whipping cream

2½ tablespoons dark unsweetened cocoa powder

¼ cup sugar

8 ounces semi-sweet chocolate, broken up

3 tablespoons unsalted butter

FOR THE CAKE

12 ounces semi-sweet or 70% cocoa chocolate, broken into pieces

12 tablespoons (1½ sticks) unsalted butter

1 tablespoon pure vanilla extract

½ teaspoon almond extract

7 tablespoons dark unsweetened cocoa

½ teaspoon ground cinnamon

6 large eggs, at room temperature

½ cup light brown sugar

I dream in dark chocolate. So vivid are my chocolate dreams, I swear I can even remember the fragrance and the texture of it on my tongue.

This dense and intensely chocolate cake is fudgelike and very moist. It is crowned with a silky chocolate ganache enhanced with Cabernet and surrounded by a raspberry Cabernet consommé. —*Hillary*

SERVES 10

1. To make the ganache, place the wine, cream, cocoa powder, and sugar in a medium saucepan and bring it to a simmer. Cook for 5 minutes. Take off the heat, add the chocolate, and stir or whisk until fully melted. Add the 3 tablespoons butter and whisk until fully melted. Scoop into a bowl, cover, and allow to sit on the counter for at least 2 hours.

2. Preheat the oven to 350°F. Butter and flour a 9-inch springform pan and line the bottom of the pan with parchment paper.

3. To make the cake, put the chocolate in a food processor and pulse until granular.

4. Melt the 12 tablespoons butter in a medium saucepan over medium heat, add the granular chocolate, and stir until the chocolate is melted and smooth. Remove the mixture from the heat and cool it for 8 minutes. Whisk in the vanilla and almond extracts, cocoa, and cinnamon.

5. Beat the eggs and brown sugar for 5 to 6 minutes on high speed with a hand mixer until increased in volume and pale yellow. Pour half the chocolate mixture in and gently fold it into the egg mixture with a rubber spatula. Add the second half of the chocolate and gently fold it into the egg mixture, trying to keep the volume intact.

6. Transfer to the springform pan, put the pan on a baking sheet and into the oven to bake for at least 40 minutes and up to 65 minutes, as it depends on the humidity in the air and the amount of liquid in your eggs. You want to take it out when it is still a little bit wobbly in the center, but cooked

on the top. It will set as it cools down. Allow the cake to cool in the pan for 45 minutes. It will deflate quite a bit.

7. Meanwhile, make the consommé. Place the raspberries, sugar, ½ cup water, and Cabernet in a medium saucepan. Use a potato masher or the back of a spoon to mash the berries into the liquid, bring to a simmer, and cook at a gentle, constant bubble for 20 to 25 minutes. The less you simmer the consommé, the thinner it will be. If you simmer it longer than 20 minutes, it will start to thicken into a syrup. It's your choice which you would prefer.

8. Strain through a fine-mesh strainer into a bowl to capture the liquid, using the back of a spoon to mash the raspberries to release all their liquid. (Keep the mashed raspberries to spread on your toast in the morning, as it will take on the attributes of jam and have an amazing flavor.)

9. After the cake has cooled in the pan for 45 minutes, undo the spring, place a plate over the top of the cake, and invert quickly. Peel off the parchment paper and leave the cake to rest for 15 minutes before frosting.

10. Frost with the ganache, slice into serving pieces, place them on plates, and spoon the consommé around the slices of cake.

STACY'S PAIRING: Wölffer Estate Vineyard Cabernet Franc, or another Cabernet Franc that was used to make the ganache, will contrast nicely with the rich sweetness of this dish.

FOR THE CONSOMMÉ
2 cups fresh raspberries
1 cup sugar
1 cup Cabernet Franc

Farmhouse Apple Pie

1 batch Miracle Piecrust (see page 142)
6 medium apples, peeled, cored, and sliced
1 cup brown sugar, packed
2 tablespoons cornstarch
1 tablespoon apple cider vinegar
1 teaspoon ground cinnamon
½ teaspoon freshly grated nutmeg
Cheddar for serving (optional)

I wasn't always an avid home cook. But when my husband and I were doing graduate studies at Stony Brook University in Stony Brook, Long Island, I got a bee in my bonnet to enter my family's apple pie in the annual apple pie contest at the historic Sherwood-Jayne Farm in East Setauket. So, I called my mom for the recipe. I didn't win the first apple pie contest I entered with Grandma Weinke's recipe, but this pie has won a few contests since then. You can add vanilla to the filling, or sanding sugar to the crust, but that's just gilding the lily. This "cheater"-pastry-meets-New-York-State-apples is the real deal.

Back on the farm we used the heirloom variety, Transparent apples, in our pies. My favorite commercially available pie apples are Pink Ladies, which I purchase from the Milk Pail Fresh Market in Water Mill. They don't fully ripen until November; in the meantime, Gravensteins from Briermere Farms in Riverhead do nicely. If you have access to organic apples, you can leave some of the skin on the fruit—less than half of it—for a somewhat heartier dish.

My family keeps the tradition of serving a small chunk of Cheddar with every slice of this pie—*mit käse,* rather than à la mode. Allow the pie to cool for at least 1 hour before serving. Cutting it while it's still hot will make the filling appear watery. —*Stacy*

SERVES 8

1. Prepare the Miracle Piecrust on page 142.

2. Preheat the oven to 400°F.

3. Mix the apples, brown sugar, cornstarch, vinegar, cinnamon, and nutmeg together in a medium mixing bowl.

4. Place the bottom crust in a 10-inch pie plate, fill it with the apple filling and cover it with the top crust. Use a fork to crimp the edges together by pressing it down along the rim of the pie plate, trimming off any excess crust. Poke several holes in the center of the top crust to vent steam. You can cut out decorative pieces of leftover crust, wet them on the back, and apply them before baking.

5. This pie will likely drip when it's baking, so wrap the pan loosely with a solid sheet of heavy-duty aluminum foil to catch any spills. Bake the pie about 1 hour 15 minutes, until the crust is golden brown.

6. Allow pie to cool for an hour or more before slicing. Serve with a piece of cheddar.

STACY'S PAIRING: Dark rum warmed over the lowest heat setting and stirred with a cinnamon stick makes for a heady accompaniment to this traditional American dish. Spicy Sag Harbor Rum works well in this preparation.

Fall Fruit Granola Crumble

There are many, many fruit crumble recipes in the world. They are probably all good, but I find that this version makes the most of blending the season's fruits with wine, and it has a savory touch. Feel free to substitute other fruits, such as peaches or blueberries. Just don't forget to pick up some local ice cream to go with this crumble. If you use a thicker-skinned pear, such as Bosc or Asian, do peel this fruit. —Stacy

SERVES 8

1. Preheat the oven to 400°F. Butter and flour a 2-quart covered casserole dish.

2. To prepare the topping, place the butter, flour, ¾ cup maple sugar, cinnamon, ginger, and pepper in a food processor and combine by pulsing until the mixture resembles coarse crumbs. Pour the crumble mixture into a mixing bowl and stir in the oats, nuts, and cheese.

3. To prepare the filling, combine the apples, pears, raspberries, ¾ cup maple sugar, red wine, cornstarch, and salt in a medium mixing bowl and stir to mix. Place the filling mixture in the baking dish.

4. Cover the filling evenly with the topping. Cover the dish and bake about 45 minutes. The filling should be bubbling vigorously.

5. Turn the oven down to 350°F.

6. Remove the dish's cover and continue baking for about 15 minutes, until the topping is golden brown.

7. Allow the crumble to cool for at least 5 minutes before serving. Serve hot or warm with ice cream or whipped cream, if using.

STACY'S PAIRING: A scoop of ice cream and a glass of sweet port, such as Sannino Vineyard Pure Profit Fortified Red Dessert Wine, do nicely with this fragrant baked dessert.

FOR THE CRUMBLE TOPPING

11 tablespoons unsalted butter, cut into chunks, plus more for the baking dish

¾ cup flour, plus more for the baking dish

¾ cup maple sugar or packed brown sugar

2 teaspoons ground cinnamon

1 teaspoon ground ginger

⅛ teaspoon freshly ground black pepper

¾ cup old-fashioned oatmeal

¾ cup sliced hazelnuts or walnuts

2 tablespoons grated extra-sharp Cheddar

FOR THE FILLING

2 tart apples cored, peeled, and chopped

2 organic Bartlett or Anjou pears, cored and chopped

1 half-pint (1 cup) raspberries

¾ cup packed maple sugar or brown sugar

2 tablespoons red wine

2 tablespoons cornstarch

¼ teaspoon sea salt

Ice cream or whipped cream (optional)

East End Cheeseboard

FOR THE CHEESEBOARD
Mecox Bay Dairy: Mecox Sigit (a firm, Alpine-style cow's milk cheese)
Mecox Bay Dairy: Atlantic Mist (a soft, brie-style cow's milk cheese)
Catapano Dairy Farm: Sundancer (a firm, romano-style sheep's milk cheese)
Catapano Dairy Farm: Feta Alfresco (a brined goat cheese)
Goodale Farms: lavender butter
Cheeseball (see below)
Fresh seasonal fruit, sliced

FOR THE CHEESEBALL
½ cup chopped fresh or dried green herbs such as parsley, basil, dill, or savory
4 ounces cream cheese
2 tablespoons Parmigiano-Reggiano
¼ teaspoon freshly ground black pepper

Ah, the cheeseboard. Traditionally served at the close of a meal, often replacing dessert, a cheeseboard can be a joy at any time—at the top of the meal, or indeed, for an intimate gathering, it can be the main attraction. Below is just one possible combination of Long Island cheeses.

On Long Island's East End we have cow, goat, and sheep cheeses. To create your own local cheeseboard, seek out different cheeses (got buffalo, moose, or reindeer cheese?) in a variety of textures, styles, and colors. I also like to include a local compound butter such as lavender or parsley, because it begs to be slathered. Offer a variety of "conveyances" as well—crackers, bread, and rusks. You want to avoid anything too flavorful that might compete with the flavors of the cheeses.

The most important element in enjoying the nuances of cheese is temperature. Bring all of the aged cheeses out of the refrigerator about an hour before they are to be served. Fresh cheeses may be served chilled. Give each cheese its own knife so that the flavors don't become mixed.

I think four different cheeses is a good number for a basic cheeseboard. To that I would suggest adding a cheeseball, some fresh fruit, and beach plum jelly or raspberry-horseradish jam. Long Islanders can never get enough of our native beach plums. Tart jellies and jams work well spread over a smear of cheeseball on a cracker.

This cheeseball recipe is super-easy and inexpensive. I guarantee that everyone who tries it will ask you where you purchased such a "fine goat cheese." You can, alternatively, roll this cheese mixture into a log rather than a ball shape. Either way, when tightly wrapped it freezes well, for up to a month. If you're going to freeze a cheeseball, use dried rather than fresh herbs to coat it; they keep better. —*Stacy*

SERVES 10

1. For the cheeseball: Place the herbs in a shallow bowl.

2. Place both cheeses and the pepper in a food processor and mix until the mixture is uniform.

3. Wet your hands and use them to form the cheese mixture into a ball. Dip the cheeseball into the bowl of herbs to coat all sides. Wrap it in waxed paper and refrigerate it until just before serving.

STACY'S PAIRING: Try a very lightly chilled extra brut sparkling wine with your cheeseboard. The wine's dryness means that there won't be fruit flavors to interfere with your experience of the cheeses.

Wölffer Estate Vineyard Rosé Sparkling Wine, Noblesse Oblige Extra Brut, made in the *méthode traditionnelle*, is exceptionally food friendly. Of course champagne-like wines love salt and fat, so cheese is a natural pairing. But I find this wine to be especially "cheese friendly" for its yeastiness and smoothness. Plus its base notes are not "fruity" but of the fruit—its delicacy just can't get in the way of any food's flavors. It's made from Pinot Noir grapes and just a smidgen of Merlot.

But a cheeseboard invites comparative analysis. How do the different cheeses taste with different wines? This is a great opportunity to bring out a wide range of wines for everyone to experiment with, including ports, other dessert wines, and Rieslings. Red wine pairs best with sharp, aged cheeses.

Chapter Five

WINTER

Thanksgiving to Easter/Passover

All but the hardiest plants take a rest as Long Island's famous bay
scallops sweeten. This is prime time for Hamptons *hygge*—for
cocooning and cooking up a winter repast.

SMALL PLATES

Clam Chowder with Parsley Butter Croutons 192
Small Cornmeal Pancakes with Beef Carpaccio 196
Individual Crudités, Cilantro Hummus, and Miso Cheddar Cookies 198
Peconic Bay Scallops with Riesling Cream 200

SALADS

Lettuce Boats with Swiss Cheese and Apples 202
Winter Sun Salad 203
Raw Roots Salad with Green Apple Vinaigrette 205

MAINS

Crunchy Mac 'n' Cheese 206
Montauk Lobster Pot Pie 208
Winter Storm Baked Fresh Ham with Mustard Sauce and Apple Chutney 210
Wine Country Beef Stew 212
Hot Lobster Rolls 215
Braised Beef Short Ribs with Botanical Gremolata 216
Slow Roasted Honeyed Chicken or Rabbit 218

DESSERTS

Windmill Cookies with Boozy Milkshakes 220
Chocolate Sauerkraut Layer Cake with Sea Salt Caramel Glaze 223
Cider-Poached Apples on a Cloud of Cider-Sweetened Ricotta 226
Warm White Chocolate Parsnip Pudding 228

FOR THE PARSLEY BUTTER CROUTONS

4 slices stale bread, cut into quarters, with or without crusts

1 packed cup parsley and other soft, green herbs such as basil, chives, cilantro, oregano

⅓ cup unsalted, clarified butter, at room temperature

2 garlic cloves, crushed in a garlic press

½ teaspoon sea salt

½ teaspoon freshly ground black pepper

⅛ teaspoon ground cayenne pepper

FOR THE CHOWDER

4 slices organic bacon

2 medium yellow onions, chopped

2 tablespoons all-purpose flour

3 cups whole milk

2 cups clam broth

3 large (1½ pounds) Yukon Gold potatoes, diced

¼ teaspoon dried lovage or celery seed

¼ teaspoon freshly ground black pepper

1 pound shucked hard-shell clams or three 6.5-ounce cans chopped clams, undrained

Clam Chowder with Parsley Butter Croutons

I've enjoyed "Long Island Clam Chowder" in restaurants across our island—usually it's red Manhattan style, made with tomatoes; and sometimes it's white New England style. I'm just going to say it—it's good both ways. The key ingredient, always, are the sweet, local chowder clams. —*Stacy*

SERVES 4

1. Preheat the oven to 400°F. Line a baking sheet with parchment paper.

2. To prepare the croutons, place the cut pieces of bread in a medium mixing bowl.

3. Place the herbs, butter, garlic, salt, ½ teaspoon pepper, and cayenne in a food processor and process until almost liquefied, about 30 seconds, scraping down the bowl as needed.

4. Pour the herb mixture over the pieces of bread and gently stir to coat them. Place the croutons on the prepared baking sheet so that they are not touching. Set aside until the chowder is cooking.

5. To make the chowder, cover a large plate with paper towels. Place the bacon in a Dutch oven, cover loosely with parchment paper, and bake about 15 minutes, until the bacon is somewhat crispy. Remove the bacon from the Dutch oven and set it aside on the prepared plate, leaving the bacon fat in the Dutch oven. Leave the oven on to bake the croutons.

6. Put the Dutch oven on a burner over medium heat. Add the onions to the bacon fat and sauté until golden, about 5 minutes. Stir the flour into the onions. Gradually add the milk and clam broth to the onions, stirring constantly. Add the potatoes, lovage, and ¼ teaspoon pepper. Cover loosely and cook until the potatoes are tender, about 15 minutes.

7. Bake the croutons in the 400°F oven for 5 minutes. Turn each crouton over and bake until golden brown, about 5 minutes more. If not using immediately, remove the croutons from the oven and rest on a cooling rack until ready to serve.

8. Coarsely chop the clam meat. Add the clams to the Dutch oven and cook until heated through, about 3 minutes.

9. Chop the bacon.

10. To serve, ladle the chowder into bowls and add 2 croutons to the top of each bowl of chowder. Sprinkle the chopped bacon over the chowder. Serve immediately.

STACY'S PAIRING: Look for an India pale ale with sweet top notes over that touch of bitter hops. The sweet-bitter balance of Oyster Bay Brewing Company IPA works well with this rich dish.

LONG ISLAND CLAM CHOWDER

Arguments abound as to which is the more authentic version of clam chowder on Long Island—red, tomato-based, or white, roux-based. For the answer, I look to the storied East Hampton Ladies' Village Improvement Society's (LVIS) cookbook circa 1965. In this, the 70th anniversary edition, it says, "Tomatoes, which we value so highly for their vitamin content and consider indispensable for salads, were considered poisonous by our early ancestors." The former LVIS president, Mrs. Nathan H. Dayton, is quoted in the text as saying that she could "remember when East Hampton people first began to eat tomatoes. The late Miss Adaline Sherrill said that her grandmother raised her tomato vines on discarded hoopskirt frames. Hoopskirts had just gone out of fashion here, when tomatoes came in."

So there you have it—Spanish and Portuguese explorers took tomatoes, a New World nightshade, to Europe in the 16th century. And they introduced the New World to dairy cows. Thomas Jefferson discovered the joys of tomatoes in France in the early 19th century and brought seeds back to grow at Monticello, but it took decades longer for tomatoes to be accepted on the East End of Long Island. —Stacy

Small Cornmeal Pancakes with Beef Carpaccio

FOR THE SWEET RED PEPPER SAUCE

2 garlic cloves

½ cup hazelnuts

½ teaspoon sea salt

1 teaspoon sugar

One 7-ounce jar roasted red peppers, drained

2 medium plum tomatoes, sliced and seeded

1 tablespoon plus 1 teaspoon sherry vinegar

¼ teaspoon red pepper flakes

1 teaspoon sweet paprika

1 slice white bread, crustless, torn into pieces

1 tablespoon extra virgin olive oil

FOR THE CARPACCIO

8 ounces sirloin beef, raw, sliced as thinly as possible

1 tablespoon extra virgin olive oil

½ teaspoon sea salt flakes

3 cracks freshly ground black pepper

The egg yolks may be refrigerated in a sealed container for up to 4 days for another use.

Living in the heart of one of the country's most popular wine regions, I love to host a wine tasting that also includes samples from our local wineries and breweries, asking my friend and coauthor, Stacy Dermont, to officiate and share her deep knowledge of Long Island libations. For the party, I serve small bites such as this one. Sometimes these are so good that, as I make them, I end up eating most of them while standing in the kitchen.

There are a few steps to making them, but each step is quick and easy. Just be sure to leave enough for your guests. —*Hillary*

SERVES 4 TO 6

1. To prepare the sweet red pepper sauce, with the food processor running, drop in the garlic, hazelnuts, salt, and sugar, and process until finely minced.

2. Add the roasted red peppers, plum tomatoes, vinegar, red pepper flakes, and paprika, and process until smooth.

3. With the processor still running, add the bread and process for 30 seconds, then add the 1 tablespoon olive oil in a thin stream until the sauce is emulsified and smooth. Reserve.

4. For the carpaccio, place each slice of beef in between two pieces of parchment paper and, with a rolling pin, hit each as gently as possible to flatten it out even thinner. Slice each one into 3-inch pieces. Drizzle them with the 1 tablespoon olive oil, salt flakes, and pepper and toss to coat. Reserve.

5. Preheat the oven to 200°F.

6. To make the pancakes, put the dry ingredients into a large mixing bowl and whisk to combine.

7. In a small saucepan, melt the butter over medium-low heat. Take off the heat and add 2 tablespoons of the oil, milk, and honey, and whisk until combined. Pour into the dry ingredients and whisk to combine.

8. In another large bowl, beat the egg whites until they hold their shape, then very gently fold them into the dough mixture.

9. Add the remaining 1 tablespoon olive oil to a griddle or large frying pan set over medium heat. Drop the batter by a level tablespoon onto the frying pan and cook the pancakes for 2 minutes, then turn over and cook for 1 minute, until golden brown on each side. Keep warm in the oven if you wish to serve them soon. Otherwise, serve at room temperature the same day.

10. To serve, arrange the beef on top of each pancake, then spoon a dollop of the sauce over the beef, garnish with a cilantro leaf, if using, and serve.

STACY'S PAIRING: Look for a hearty, robust amber ale, like Blue Point Brewing Company Winter Ale, to stand up to the rich and complex flavors in this dish.

FOR THE PANCAKES

1 cup organic fine grind cornmeal

½ cup rice flour

1½ teaspoons sea salt

1 teaspoon baking powder

¼ teaspoon ground cumin

2 tablespoons unsalted butter

3 tablespoons olive oil

1 cup milk or almond milk

2 tablespoons honey

2 large egg whites, at room temperature

Cilantro leaves for garnish (optional)

Individual Crudités, Cilantro Hummus, and Miso Cheddar Cookies

FOR THE COOKIES

8 ounces extra-sharp Cheddar

6 tablespoons unsalted butter, at room temperature

2 large egg yolks

¾ teaspoon red miso paste

6 cracks freshly ground black pepper

2 sprigs fresh thyme, leaves only, plus more for garnish

¼ teaspoon cayenne pepper

1 tablespoon toasted sesame seeds

1⅓ cups flour

1 egg yolk mixed with 1 teaspoon water for egg wash

Herbs, sesame seeds, sea salt flakes for garnish (optional)

FOR THE HUMMUS

Two 15-ounce cans chickpeas, drained

4 cups tightly packed fresh cilantro leaves, plus more for garnish

2 large garlic cloves, sliced

2 teaspoons sea salt

1 lemon, juiced

½ cup extra virgin olive oil

The plates were all different, found at weekend antique shows and flea markets. Down the center of the table was a long runner holding two oval containers with great bouquets of winter vegetables and vases filled with flowers, a veritable indoor garden mixing up vegetables with flowers. Smaller bowls of dips were nearby, a wooden cutting board crowned with a pile of small baguettes, and white ceramic ramekins of perfectly leveled sweet butter.

Outside, snow piled under a big black sky. Inside, the crackling from the fireplace warmed us. We were dining in a fabulous modern house built to mimic the low-lying potato barns that dot the Hamptons landscape. The house had its own wing for entertaining, and at its heart a fabulous kitchen and this long formal stone table we were sitting at.

It was a night and a meal to remember, inspiration to create my own smaller version at home. Each guest at my table will find their own antique plate or cutting board filled with a selection of winter vegetables, or simply with a few lovely carrots and dips. The only two things to make are the Cheddar cookies and cilantro hummus. —*Hillary*

SERVES 4 TO 6

1. On the big holes of a box grater, grate the Cheddar into the bowl of a food processor.

2. Add the butter, egg yolks, miso paste, pepper, thyme, cayenne, and sesame seeds and process until mixed and creamy.

3. Add the flour and process until granular. Then, with the machine running, slowly add 2 tablespoons ice water until the dough just comes together.

4. Scoop out the dough onto a large piece of parchment paper and bring it together with your hands, squeezing and kneading it a little to eliminate any cracks and so that it looks smooth. Roll it into two logs about 2 inches thick, wrap tightly in parchment paper, and place in the refrigerator for 1 hour.

5. Preheat the oven to 325°F. Line two baking sheets with parchment paper.

6. Run a sharp knife under hot water, then slice each log into ¼-inch discs and place slices on the prepared baking sheets, about 1 inch apart. Place in the freezer for 15 minutes while the oven preheats.

7. When ready to bake, take the cookies out of the freezer, paint them with the egg wash, then decorate with herbs or sesame seeds or sea salt flakes, if you wish.

8. Bake the cheddar cookies 13 to 20 minutes, or until the cookies are turning golden brown on top. Timing will depend on the width and the thickness of the cookies, so keep an eye on them. Cool on a wire rack.

9. To make the hummus, add all the hummus ingredients into the bowl of a food processor and process until smooth and creamy. Scoop into small, individual serving bowls and garnish with cilantro leaves.

The egg whites may be refrigerated in a sealed container for up to 4 days for another use.

STACY'S PAIRING: This dish has a lot of culinary bells and whistles. It wants for a clean, very versatile white wine. Macari Vineyards Chardonnay is just such a quaff.

Peconic Bay Scallops with Riesling Cream

FOR THE SCALLOPS

3 tablespoons unsalted butter

1 tablespoon olive oil

1 pound bay scallops, rinsed and patted very dry

½ organic lemon, finely zested

Sea salt flakes to taste

¼ cup minced flat parsley leaves

FOR THE RIESLING CREAM

2 cups dry Riesling

1 shallot, minced

2 tablespoons unsalted butter

1 tablespoon heavy whipping cream

Sea salt to taste

How to say goodbye to winter? Wait until February, when it's really cold. Have friends over for dinner. Find daffodils. They will offer hope. Score some Peconic Bay scallops. They will be a treat. Offer a huge bowl generously over-filled with pasta tossed in buttery Riesling cream. That will fill people up and make them happy. End of winter, hello spring. —*Hillary*

SERVES 4

1. To perfectly cook tiny bay scallops takes three steps. First, get a large frying pan hot before you add the 3 tablespoons butter and oil. Second, add the butter and oil and heat it until it begins to get bubbly. Third, add the scallops and pan fry them over medium-high heat until golden brown on all sides, about 30 seconds. Since you can safely eat scallops raw, remember to not overcook them, looking only for a good golden sear and a center that is just translucent. Drain on paper towels.

2. For the Riesling cream, over medium heat, deglaze the same frying pan with the wine, add the shallot, and bring to a boil, reduce to a simmer, cooking for about 5 minutes. Add the 2 tablespoons butter, cream, and salt to taste, and whisk until blended.

3. To serve, divide the scallops equally onto the center of each plate, garnish with lemon zest and sea salt flakes. Spoon the sauce around the scallops and scatter the minced parsley over the scallops.

STACY'S PAIRING: A dry, sharp Chardonnay could work with this creamy dish, but I quite like Castello di Borghese Vineyard and Winery Barrel Fermented Chardonnay, a rich mid-palate white that boasts a creamy finish.

PECONIC BAY SCALLOPS

Thimble-sized pearls of sweetness, our Peconic Bay scallops, *Argopecten irradians*, are available in limited quantity, in part due to the same algae blooms that have crippled our oyster and clam populations since 1985. If you are lucky enough to find fresh ones at your fish market, usually from the first Monday in November through March 31, scoop them up and bring them home. Because they are scarce and labor-intensive to harvest during the freezing temperatures of winter, they are expensive for good reason.

Make sure you are buying ones labeled Peconic Bay scallops, because if they are labeled bay scallops, they are harvested from coastal waters in the south, and all the way to Maine, and have endured shipping and possibly had the food additive sodium tripolyphosphate (STP) added to them to increase their weight and to keep them from drying out. These often exhibit an other-worldly white color.

To cook our local tiny bay scallops, simply rinse them under cold water and pat very dry. Pan fry quickly over medium-high heat and make every effort to not overcook them as they can be eaten raw and do not require much more than a sear. —*Hillary*

Lettuce Boats with Swiss Cheese and Apples

FOR THE VINAIGRETTE

¼ cup extra virgin olive oil

1 tablespoon apple cider vinegar

2 teaspoons honey

½ teaspoon Dijon mustard

¼ teaspoon sea salt

FOR THE SALAD

1 large leaf from a red cabbage, sliced into matchsticks

2 organic Honeycrisp apples, unpeeled, sliced into matchsticks

Four ¼-inch slices Swiss cheese, sliced into matchsticks

4 rainbow chard stems, sliced into matchsticks

4 ounces golden raisins

8 large romaine lettuce leaves

On a walk through an orchard market still open in the middle of winter, I saw pale green apples lined up in a column. They were cold to the touch, and not much else was on offer. The cashier stomped her feet and blew on her fingertips to keep warm as she bagged them for me.

My thought for making salad that night changed. Rather than a rambunctious riot of colorful ingredients, I would instead make a pale green and monastic white salad.

I picked up my bag and took the apples home. A big head of lettuce provided my boats. Other good things came effortlessly together. So many times for me, recipes are created with what is at hand. This salad surprised me, every delicious crunchy bite. —*Hillary*

SERVES 4

1. Whisk together the ingredients for the vinaigrette in a medium bowl. Add the red cabbage, apples, cheese, chard stems, and golden raisins, and toss well to coat.

2. Arrange two romaine leaves on each plate, one tucked right behind the other. Using tongs or two forks, arrange the tossed ingredients inside each leaf and serve.

STACY'S PAIRING: A somewhat tart Pinot Grigio melds with the touch of mustard and bite of apple in this dish. Locally, Suhru Wines, Pinot Grigio fits this bill of fare.

Winter Sun Salad

While snowed-in last winter, I decided to make a dish to brighten things up. What's local and colorful on cold days? Squash! I had a store of them at hand. I decided that slices of butternut squash would make perfect "flames" around a tasty sun, though acorn squash would certainly work. Neither need be peeled for this recipe.

This Italian vinaigrette, my standard dressing for tossed salads, also works as a marinade for grilling. Though I sometimes blend my own herbs to create an Italian seasoning mix, I quite like the Italian seasoning from Citarella in Bridgehampton, which includes oregano, basil, marjoram, and rosemary.

This recipe can be doubled and quadrupled. Store vinaigrette in the refrigerator between uses. —*Stacy*

SERVES 4

1. Place all the vinaigrette ingredients in a sealable jar and shake to combine. Add salt to taste.

2. Preheat the oven to 400°F. Line two baking sheets with parchment paper and coat the paper with oil.

3. Place the feta and ½ cup of the Italian vinaigrette in a resealable pint container and shake to coat. Allow the cheese to marinate at room temperature as you prepare the other salad components.

4. Wash the squash. Lay it on its side on a cutting board and slice off the stem end. Cut the squash crosswise to remove its long neck from its bulbous bottom. Cut the bottom in half lengthwise and scoop out the seeds with a spoon. Place the seeds in a cup with 2 tablespoons of olive oil and stir to coat. Cut the squash neck in half lengthwise. Slice the neck and the seeded bottom halves into crescents about ¼ inch thick. Place the squash slices on the oiled parchment. Then turn all the squash slices over, so both sides are oiled. Sprinkle the squash slices with ground black pepper and place them in the oven.

5. Bake the squash for 10 minutes, turn the slices over, and bake about 10 minutes more, until cooked through. Remove the pans from the oven.

6. Turn the oven down to 325°F.

Continued . . .

FOR THE EASY ITALIAN VINAIGRETTE
¾ cup olive oil
¼ cup apple cider vinegar
1 teaspoon Italian seasoning
1 teaspoon maple syrup
½ teaspoon freshly ground black pepper
Sea salt to taste

FOR THE SALAD
5 ounces feta, crumbled
1 large butternut squash
4 tablespoons olive oil
Freshly ground black pepper to taste
Amagansett Sea Salt or other finishing salt to taste
2 garlic cloves, coarsely chopped
8 ounces kale or chard, coarsely chopped and rinsed
1 tablespoon apple cider vinegar

7. Spread the seeds on a fresh sheet of parchment on one of the pans and salt liberally. Bake for 10 minutes, then turn the seeds over and bake about 10 minutes more, until the seeds are lightly browned. Remove the pan from the oven and remove the parchment paper the seeds are on from the pan, to halt their cooking.

8. Heat the remaining 2 tablespoons of the olive oil in a medium frying pan over medium heat. Add the garlic and cook it until it's fragrant and softening, about 2 minutes.

9. Sauté the damp kale in the olive oil and garlic until tender, about 15 minutes. Stir in the vinegar. Divide the cooked greens among the serving dishes. Arrange the squash crescents around the edge of each plate or bowl. Divide the marinated feta among the dishes, centering it on the greens. Sprinkle the seeds over the salads. Serve immediately.

STACY'S PAIRING: The pronounced vinegar aspect of this dish favors beer over wine. Try a German-style lager or Greenport Harbor Brewing Company Tidal Lager, which tastes of lightly toasted malt with a hint of nuttiness.

Raw Roots Salad with Green Apple Vinaigrette

Alchemy is about taking something ugly or considered of little value and making something beautiful or valuable out of it. Consider the humble beet. It's a root vegetable with exquisite earthy sweet flavor that's just begging for the wave of a wand and a little magic. And talk about ugly—celeriac (celery root) must certainly win the prize. Add to these "beauties" some crisp, sweet carrots and radishes and you have a pretty, crunchy, colorful salad packed with flavor and nutrition.

To attain a pleasing and uniform consistency, grate all the vegetables on the big holes of a box grater. —Hillary

SERVES 4

1. To make the vinaigrette, put all the vinaigrette ingredients into a food processor and blend. Add a little water if you would like it thinner.

2. Add all the salad ingredients into a big serving bowl, pour the vinaigrette over, and toss to thoroughly coat before heaping it into a large serving bowl.

STACY'S PAIRING: This mix of ingredients calls for a beer with a versatile flavor profile, something kind of "warm" in contrast to "raw," like a mild lager such as Moustache Brewing Company Same As It Ever Was pale lager.

FOR THE VINAIGRETTE

1 small Granny Smith apple, peeled, cored, and sliced
½ cup olive oil
¼ cup apple cider vinegar
1 tablespoon minced shallot
1 teaspoon sugar
¼ teaspoon sea salt

FOR THE SALAD

2 cups grated raw beets
1 cup grated raw celeriac
1 cup grated raw carrots
1 cup grated raw radishes
1 cup arugula
2 tablespoons finely chopped red onion
¼ cup golden raisins
¼ cup finely chopped mint leaves
½ cup finely chopped hazelnuts

Clean mint trimmings may be used to make a tisane.

Healthy radish greens may be used to make the Radish Greens Pesto over a Tangle of Pasta on page 40.

Crunchy Mac 'n' Cheese

2 cups cooked winter squash pulp (see page 181) or 1 large acorn squash, if using

1 cup grated sharp Cheddar

2 tablespoons grated Pecorino Romano

¾ cup vegetable or chicken stock

¼ cup yogurt, ricotta, or cream cheese

1 teaspoon Dijon mustard

1 teaspoon bottled horse-radish

½ teaspoon kosher salt

¼ teaspoon ground cayenne pepper

1½ cups rotini or other medium-sized pasta

2 cups chopped romanesque or cauliflower florets

Butter, to grease the baking pan

½ cup corn bread crumbs

Leftover cooked squash pulp can be covered and frozen for up to one year.

If you've used a butternut squash, you may prepare the seeds as you would pumpkin seeds, as detailed in the recipe for Quick-Pickled Pumpkin Salad with Candied Pumpkin Seeds on page 160.

My family loves macaroni and cheese, especially when the nights are cold. We love our winter squash too. I was inspired by a Weight Watchers recipe to combine the two—the squash adds flavor and color. I prefer corn bread crumbs for this dish, but regular bread crumbs will work. —Stacy

SERVES 4

1. Place the squash pulp, cheeses, stock, yogurt, mustard, horseradish, salt, and cayenne in a food processor and whiz until smooth—some small chunks of squash are okay.

2. Preheat the oven to 350°F. Butter a 9-by-13-inch baking pan.

3. Bring water to a boil in a large saucepan over medium-high heat. Cook the pasta for 5 minutes. Add the romanesque and continue to cook for 1 minute. Drain and place the pasta mixture in the prepared pan.

4. Pour the squash sauce over the pasta mixture to cover. Sprinkle the corn bread crumbs over the top.

5. Bake until the top is starting to brown, about 20 minutes. Serve hot or warm.

STACY'S PAIRING: Just as apple pie loves Cheddar, so does apple cider. Woodside Orchards' traditional hard cider is a great fit for this cheesy dish.

Montauk Lobster Pot Pie

Four 1¼-pound fresh live
lobsters
½ cup lobster juice, from the
cooked lobsters
1 package frozen puff pastry
1 medium russet potato
3 tablespoons extra virgin
olive oil
2 small shallots, minced
2 garlic cloves, minced
1 tablespoon unsalted butter
5 tablespoons plus 2 tea-
spoons flour
2 cups fish stock
½ cup plus 1 teaspoon dry
sherry
1 teaspoon sea salt
½ teaspoon sweet paprika
½ cup heavy cream
2 sprigs fresh tarragon,
leaves only, minced
4 ounces Gruyère, grated
2 cups frozen mixed peas
and carrots, defrosted

When the urge for lobster arises, I make a lobster pot pie like this one. It's a bit extravagant, as each pot pie requires the meat of one whole lobster.

Don't use store-bought, prepared lobster meat, as it will become too tough. This recipe intentionally undercooks the lobster meat before it is placed in the pies. I serve these in four 10-ounce ramekins or baking dishes, and I typically use store-bought frozen buttery puff pastry to top them. —*Hillary*

MAKES FOUR 10-OUNCE POT PIES

1. Put 2 large pots of salted water on the stove and bring to a rolling boil. Drop 2 lobsters into each pot, head first, and continue to boil for 5 minutes. Use tongs to remove them and place them in a colander. Run cold water over them to cool them down.

2. Hold the lobsters over a bowl as you remove the meat so that you catch any lobster juice to use later. Crack the lobsters' claws to remove the meat and place it in a medium bowl. Slice the tails down the middle and pull out the meat and add that to the bowl. Remove as much meat as you can from the lobsters and when you get to the legs, pull them off and roll a rolling pin over them to extract the meat. Once all the meat is out, slice it into small pieces and divide it evenly among the four ramekins. Pour the lobster juice into a measuring cup.

3. Thaw the puff pastry according to package instructions.

4. Slice the potato into quarters. Put them in a medium saucepan, cover with water, place on medium heat, and cook until just tender, about 8 minutes, but not falling apart. Cool, then slice the potatoes into small pieces and evenly divide them among four 10-ounce ramekins.

5. Heat the oil in a large saucepan then add the shallots and garlic and cook until tender, about 3 minutes. Add the butter; when it has melted, sprinkle in the flour, whisk, and cook for a couple of minutes.

6. Add the fish stock and lobster juice and whisk and cook until thickened. Add the sherry, salt, paprika, cream, and tarragon and whisk to blend. Stir in the cheese and stir until melted. Stir in the peas and carrots. Keep warm.

7. Preheat the oven to 400°F.

8. Roll out each piece of thawed puff pastry enough so that you can cut two tops from each sheet to put on top of the ramekins.

9. Put the ramekins on the rimmed baking sheet. Divide the warm sauce among the four ramekins. Top with the puff pastry tops. Bake for 15 to 20 minutes or until golden. Serve immediately.

STACY'S PAIRING: The tarragon and seafood aspects of this dish demand an uncomplicated, light wine like Duck Walk Vineyards Southampton White, which is made from Cayuga grapes.

Winter Storm Baked Fresh Ham with Mustard Sauce and Apple Chutney

One 10- to 15-pound fresh, uncured, bone-in ham
Whole cloves (at least 3 tablespoons, depending on size of ham)
½ cup ruby port

FOR THE GLAZE
2 cups ruby port
¼ cup honey
¼ cup light brown sugar
10 whole cloves
3 teaspoons Dijon mustard
¼ teaspoon sea salt

FOR THE MUSTARD SAUCE
2 cups half-and-half
2 large egg yolks, beaten
¾ cup light brown sugar
½ cup plus 2 tablespoons apple cider vinegar
¼ cup dry mustard
3 tablespoons honey
3 tablespoons ruby port
2 tablespoons flour
1 tablespoon Dijon mustard
1 teaspoon turmeric powder
¼ teaspoon sea salt

Before the first flurries are expected on a cold wintry weekend, I invite a crowd and bake a big fresh ham for them. It is a low-maintenance, stress-free operation that takes little preparation yet provides maximum comfort and applause. Once it is in the oven it leaves me hours to do other things, like read a book, watch a movie, or play with my dog Lilly.

I serve this roast, crowning the center of the table, with a choice of two condiments, a tangy creamy mustard sauce and an apple chutney.

Make sure to special order your ham a couple days in advance from a local farm or butcher. Any leftovers of ham are gold for making morning hash or awesome sandwiches. Use the bone and trimmings to make split pea soup. —Hillary

SERVES 8 TO 12

1. Two hours before roasting, take the ham out of the refrigerator. Rinse, pat dry, and leave to come to room temperature.

2. Place one rack in the bottom of the oven. Preheat the oven to 450°F.

3. Using a small sharp knife, score the skin on the ham with cross-hatches to create diamond patterns, then insert one whole clove at the center of each diamond.

4. Put the ham on a rack in a roasting pan, fat side up. If you have an oven-safe thermometer, insert it into the center of the ham, being careful not to touch the bone. Roast the ham in the oven for 30 minutes. Reduce the heat to 350°F. Pour ½ cup of port over the ham and return it to the oven.

5. The ham will need to cook about 18 to 20 minutes a pound, so halfway through, cover the ham with a tent of aluminum foil and, 30 minutes before taking it out, begin to glaze it as follows.

6. To make the glaze, put all the glaze ingredients into a medium saucepan and cook over high heat until it thickens, approximately 15 minutes, whisking frequently. Remove the cloves from the glaze and discard. Brush the ham all over with half the glaze, return it to the oven and bake for 15 min-

utes, uncovered. Take out the ham, brush it over with the remaining glaze, and return to bake for another 15 minutes, uncovered.

7. If you don't have an oven-safe thermometer, insert an instant-read thermometer and when it reads a minimum of 145°F, remove the ham from the oven, put the foil tent over the top, and allow to rest for 30 minutes before carving.

8. To make the mustard sauce, add the half-and-half and egg yolks to a medium saucepan and whisk well to combine. Add all the other mustard sauce ingredients, whisk over medium heat until bubbles begin to form and the sauce has thickened. Turn off the heat and cover to keep it warm.

9. To make the chutney, heat the olive oil in a medium saucepan, then add the onion and cook over medium heat for about 5 minutes, until softened. Add the apples, ginger, salt, sugars, vinegar, cranberries, and ¼ cup water, then cover and cook for about 6 minutes, until the apples have softened. Sprinkle on the cornstarch and cook, stirring constantly, until thickened. Remove from the heat and cool to room temperature.

10. To carve the ham, slice off enough on the bottom so that the ham will sit securely on a cutting board. Stick a large fork into the ham to hold it, and with a long sharp knife in your other hand, slice down to the bone for each slice. I like lovely thin slices arranged on a serving platter with a bowl of the chutney and a sauce boat holding the warm mustard sauce.

STACY'S PAIRING: A silky, oaked Chardonnay like Palmer Vineyards Old Roots Chardonnay adds another dimension of flavor to this dish.

FOR THE CHUTNEY

2 tablespoons olive oil

1 medium red onion, small dice

7 Granny Smith apples, peeled, ½-inch dice

1 teaspoon freshly grated ginger

½ teaspoon sea salt

½ cup sugar

½ cup light brown sugar

¼ cup apple cider vinegar

½ cup dried cranberries

2 teaspoons cornstarch

The egg whites may be refrigerated in a sealed container for up to 4 days for another use.

Wine Country Beef Stew

2½ cups wheat berries

3 pounds beef stew meat, cut into bite-size pieces

¼ cup olive oil

2 tablespoons unsalted butter, duck fat, or lard, melted

2 garlic cloves, crushed in a garlic press

1 teaspoon dried thyme

1 teaspoon sea salt

¼ teaspoon freshly ground nutmeg

¼ teaspoon freshly ground black pepper

1 ounce dried mushrooms, such as portabella or porcini

4 medium potatoes, peeled and diced

4 medium carrots, cut into bite-size chunks

4 shallots, quartered

2 medium yellow onions, quartered

1 bay leaf

1¼ cups red wine

½ cup brandy, such as Wölffer Estate Vineyard Brandy

½ teaspoon kosher salt

1½ tablespoons cornstarch

3 tablespoons unsalted butter, at room temperature

Fresh parsley for garnish

Maura Feeney, the Local History Librarian at the Montauk Library, introduced me to the Montauk Christmas Pie, also known as the Montauk Meat Pie. It traveled down from D'Escousse, Cape Breton, Nova Scotia, with fishermen who came to work Montauk waters. They exchanged these pies with their neighbors at Christmas and ate them after midnight mass.

Local historian and photographer Dell Cullum calls it a Canadian Meat Pie. His mother, Emily Burke Cullum, made many such pies from her grandmother Minnie Pitts's recipe of cubed beef, salt pork, onion, a basic crust, and salt and pepper. Life was hard in Montauk, so this meat pie was a real celebration.

I decided to lose the crust and "wine it up" for the modern palate. You can reduce the amount of meat to 2 pounds and increase the total amount of carrots and potatoes by 1 pound for a somewhat lighter—but still hearty—stew. —Stacy

SERVES 6

1. Soak the wheat berries in a nonreactive pot filled with water for at least 6 hours.

2. Remove the meat from the refrigerator to rest at room temperature for about 30 minutes.

3. Preheat the oven to 350°F.

4. Place the olive oil and the 2 tablespoons butter or fat in a large heavy pot or Dutch oven. Add the meat and stir to coat. Stir in the garlic, thyme, sea salt, nutmeg, and pepper. Add the mushrooms, potatoes, carrots, shallots, and onions and stir to mix. Add the bay leaf. Pour in the wine and brandy.

5. Put the lid on the pot and cook the stew in the oven for 30 minutes. Reduce the heat to 325°F and cook for 3 hours.

6. About 1 hour before the stew will be done cooking, prepare the wheat berries. Add the kosher salt to their pot and boil them in their soaking water until tender, about 40 minutes.

7. When the stew is done cooking, remove it from the oven, but leave the oven on. Use a fork to mash the cornstarch into the 3 tablespoons butter in

a mug. Stir the cornstarch mixture into the stew about a quarter at a time. Cover the stew and place it in the oven to reheat for 5 minutes.

8. Drain the wheat berries and portion some of them among the serving plates, then ladle the hot stew over them, removing the bay leaf. Garnish with parsley and serve.

STACY'S PAIRING: More of that red wine. In other words, this pairing is "built in"—whatever wine you chose to use in this stew, serve more of that alongside. I tend to use Sannino Vineyard Syrah, but a Pinot Noir, a Gamay, or a Cabernet Sauvignon, all work well.

Alternatively, you might serve a full-bodied, oaked Chardonnay, which could resonate with the brandy.

Hot Lobster Rolls

If you enjoy a lobster roll and a cold brew by the beach, by all means, sidle up to one of our seafood shacks, or trucks, come summer. But in my opinion, the best season for cooking—and eating—lobster at home is in the winter months, when this crustacean is at its plumpest and heating up the kitchen is a good thing.

Hot, buttery lobster rolls are named for our neighbor across Long Island Sound. They're called "Connecticut lobster rolls."

I've always liked the idea of stuffing a delicacy into a hot dog bun—it's as great a match as champagne and cheap pizza. In fact, I like this lobster even better on slider buns, served as an appetizer—no waiting!

Speaking of cheap, this same recipe also works well with luscious shrimp—if those are local in your neck of the woods. —Stacy

MAKES 4 LOBSTER ROLLS

1. Combine the butter, paprika, mustard, and salt in a small saucepan over low heat. Stir in the vinegar. Gently stir in the cooked lobster meat to coat it and heat it through. Gently stir in the chives.

2. Fill the buns with the lobster mixture. Garnish with more fresh chives and serve immediately.

STACY'S PAIRING: Though Sancerre is considered a quintessential wine of summer, a Sauvignon Blanc that brings to mind the acidity and minerality of a Sancerre, such as Palmer Vineyards Sauvignon Blanc, brings just the right balance to this rich seafood dish. Its dry character allows the natural sweetness of the lobster to sing. (In the Sancerre wine region in France's Loire Valley the white wines are made exclusively from Sauvignon Blanc.)

6 tablespoons unsalted butter, melted
$\frac{1}{4}$ teaspoon smoked paprika
$\frac{1}{4}$ teaspoon dried mustard
$\frac{1}{4}$ teaspoon fine sea salt
2 teaspoons rice vinegar
Two $1\frac{1}{4}$-pound lobsters, cooked (to total over 1 pound of meat; see page 102)
1 tablespoon chopped fresh chives, plus more for garnish
4 hot dog buns

Braised Beef Short Ribs with Botanical Gremolata

FOR THE SHORT RIBS

3 tablespoons olive oil, more if needed

Sea salt and freshly ground black pepper to taste

8 beef short ribs

3 medium shallots, minced

3 garlic cloves, minced

2 leeks, light green part only, sliced thinly

4 large carrots, 2 minced, 2 sliced into ½-inch pieces

6 sprigs fresh thyme, leaves only

1 sprig fresh rosemary, leaves only, chopped

5 cups bold red wine

3 tablespoons tomato paste

1 whole head of garlic, sliced in half horizontally

One 16-ounce package pappardelle noodles

2 tablespoons cognac

2 tablespoons unsalted butter

Classically dark on a white plate, with only buttered noodles and freshly chopped aromatic herbs over the top, tender falling-apart beef short ribs are a superb dinner party dish. When served with a very good bottle of red wine, these ribs provide all the comfort food needed to warm a winter's night.

I usually serve them on Saturday, which is often the time I can slow down and savor shopping for and putting together a dish like this. I let it cook during the afternoon so that it can be ready for guests when they arrive in the evening. The smell of cooking with wine fills the house and is a warm welcome —*Hillary*

SERVES 4

1. Preheat the oven to 375°F.

2. Heat the 3 tablespoons oil over medium heat in a large sturdy, oven-ready pot, such as a Dutch oven, until the oil shimmers.

3. Salt and pepper the short ribs. Add them to the pot on the stove and brown on all sides for 6 minutes, turning with tongs. Remove to a plate.

4. Add more oil to the pot, if needed, heat again, then add the shallots and minced garlic and cook on medium for about 2 minutes. Add 1 of the sliced leeks, 1 of the minced carrots, the thyme, and rosemary. Layer the meat on top, then add 4 cups of the wine, the tomato paste, and enough water, if needed, to cover the meat. Slip the sliced head of garlic halves down in under the wine.

5. Cover the pot and put it in the oven to cook for 1 hour. Carefully remove the pot from the oven, uncover it and turn the ribs over, cover the pot again, and cook for another 1½ hours, adding a bit more water if needed to cover the meat.

6. Remove the pot from the oven. Take the meat out of the pot and place it on a plate. Pour the pan sauce through a sieve over a bowl to capture the liquid. Pour this liquid back into the pot. Squeeze the roasted garlic from its skin into the liquid, discarding the skins. Add the meat back in the pot,

add the reserved sliced carrots and remaining sliced leeks, place on the stove, bring to a boil, reduce to a simmer, and cook uncovered for another 30 minutes, or until the meat is fork tender.

7. Cook the egg noodles according to package directions and keep them warm until serving.

8. Make the gremolata by putting the basil, tarragon, dandelion, mint, 3 garlic cloves, ½ teaspoon salt, and grated orange peel in a food processor and process until minced. Scoop the mixture into a bowl then stir in the ½ cup olive oil.

9. Take the meat out of the pot and place it on a plate. Reduce the sauce by one-third by vigorously simmering over medium-high heat. Add the final cup of wine, cognac, and butter and whisk until the butter is melted and the sauce is glossy.

10. To serve, mound the noodles in the center of each plate, arrange 2 ribs over them, ladle the sauce over the top, and sprinkle the gremolata over each dish.

STACY'S PAIRING: Wölffer Estate Vineyard Fatalis Fatum has the tannins to stand up to the beef, and its dark but playful purple fruit notes naturally embrace the sweetness of the orange. It's a blend of Merlot, Cabernet Sauvignon, and Cabernet Franc grapes. *Fatalis fatum* means "the decision is final," so there you have it.

FOR THE GREMOLATA
½ cup tightly packed basil leaves

¼ cup tightly packed tarragon leaves

¼ cup tightly packed dandelion leaves

¼ cup tightly packed mint leaves

3 garlic cloves

½ teaspoon sea salt

2 tablespoons grated organic orange peel

½ cup extra virgin olive oil

Slow Roasted Honeyed Chicken or Rabbit

5 tablespoons unsalted butter, melted

⅓ cup honey

2 tablespoons dry mustard

1 teaspoon kosher salt

1 teaspoon freshly ground black pepper

1 teaspoon curry powder

½ cup rabbit or chicken stock, if preparing rabbit

1 chicken, or white rabbit, skinned and cut into standard pieces

It's no wonder that rabbit is making a comeback in the United States. It's tender, tasty, and inexpensive.

This is one of my great-grandmother Mildred "Granny Woody" Woodruff's recipes. People are always amused that she specifies a white rabbit. I think it's to note that this calls for a domesticated rabbit, rather than the gamier, wild brown variety.

Granny Woody was fond of cooking rabbit in many forms. Once, when I was six years old, I asked her what was cooking in her stew pot and she said, "The Easter Bunny!" I like to think that she's still laughing about the look on my face that day. —*Stacy*

SERVES 4

1. Preheat the oven to 400°F.

2. Stir the melted butter, honey, mustard, salt, pepper, and curry powder together in a small bowl.

3. Add the stock to a 10-by-14-inch baking pan, only if preparing rabbit. Arrange the chicken or rabbit in the baking pan. Pour the butter mixture over the meat to coat it.

4. Place the pan in the oven. After 20 minutes, baste the meat with the pan juices.

5. Bake for about 40 minutes total, until the chicken reaches an internal temperature of 165°F (or the rabbit reaches an internal temperature of 160°F) when measured by an instant-read thermometer inserted into the thickest part of the thigh, but not touching bone.

6. Serve hot or cold—this dish travels well for picnicking, though it is a bit sticky.

STACY'S PAIRING: This dish is mild and sweet, and it has something of an Old World feeling about it. If you're a fan of mead, you might enjoy a chilled goblet of light mead with this meat dish. Locally, W A Meadwerks in Lindenhurst offers a wide selection of this ancient fermented honey drink, from savory to very sweet.

Chef Arie Pavlou of Bistro Été in Water Mill taught me a trick for "instant mead": Gently heat 6 ounces of any tannic red wine and stir in a teaspoon of honey until it dissolves. He demonstrated this bit of music using a Burgundy. I've come to favor Sangiovese for this practice.

Windmill Cookies with Boozy Milkshakes

FOR THE COOKIES

3¾ cups flour, more if needed

1½ teaspoons baking powder

½ teaspoon fine sea salt

1 teaspoon ground cinnamon

½ pound (2 sticks) unsalted butter, at room temperature

1½ cups sugar, more for dusting

2 large eggs, beaten

1 teaspoon pure vanilla extract

½ teaspoon almond extract

Milk for brushing cookies (optional)

FOR THE MILKSHAKES

2½ pints vanilla ice cream, slightly softened

8 ounces Long Island o'Old-Tymer Whiskey or another variety of corn whiskey

¼ cup whole milk

Whipped cream

4 maraschino cherries

Inspired by the iconic boozy milkshakes they whiz up at LT Burger in Sag Harbor, I started spiking the milkshakes I make at home for friends and serving them with these Windmill Cookies, in homage to the much-adored windmills of the Hamptons. My typically unquenchable guests often ask for seconds. If your guests are like mine, you might want to have enough ingredients on hand to make more. If dessert comes first, this would be the one I would choose. —*Hillary*

MAKES 12 COOKIES AND 4 MILKSHAKES

1. Sift the flour and baking powder into a large bowl. Sprinkle in the salt and cinnamon and whisk to combine.

2. Put the butter into the bowl of a stand mixer and beat the butter until fluffy. Add the sugar and beat again. Add the eggs, vanilla, and almond extracts and beat to combine. With the machine running on low, add half the flour mixture, then the rest of the flour mixture until just combined.

3. Scoop the dough out onto a large piece of parchment paper. Bring it together with your hands, form it into a flattened disk, divide into two, then wrap each in parchment and refrigerate for 30 minutes.

4. Preheat the oven to 375°F. Line two baking sheets with parchment paper.

5. Flour a clean surface and a rolling pin. Remove the dough from the refrigerator, unwrap both pieces. Let them rest for 10 minutes if they are too hard to roll out. Knead the portions of dough to make it pliable, sprinkling more flour if needed to make the dough easier to work. Then roll each out to ¼-inch thickness.

6. Cut the cookies out with a windmill-shaped cookie cutter and place them 2 inches apart on the prepared baking sheets. (I like brushing them with milk and sprinkling with sugar, but that is optional.) Place in the oven to bake for 8 to 10 minutes, until lightly golden around the edges. Let the cookies cool.

7. While the cookies bake, or before serving, place the milkshake glasses in the freezer to chill.

8. Make the milkshakes. Do this in two batches. Put half of the ice cream in a blender, add 4 ounces whisky, $\frac{1}{8}$ cup milk, and blend. Pour or scoop into the two chilled glasses and put them in the refrigerator. Repeat this process.

9. Top each glass with whipped cream and a cherry, and serve with the windmill cookies.

STACY'S PAIRING: No pairing for this recipe—it's boozy enough on its own!

HAMPTONS WINDMILLS

By most accounts, the Hamptons has more windmills than any other region in the United States, making the windmill an iconic and much-loved symbol of our agricultural heritage. There are 11 of them currently dotting the landscape.

Our 18th- and 19th-century wooden windmills were gristmills where local farmers would come to grind their corn, wheat, and oats. They also functioned as a village gathering point for people to meet and socialize.

Rustic and whimsical, the windmills provided economical wind-driven power and are forerunners of today's electricity-generating wind turbines. —Hillary

Chocolate Sauerkraut Layer Cake with Sea Salt Caramel Glaze

My family no longer makes sauerkraut every fall; luckily, farmer Hal Goodale does. I buy his excellent kraut from the Goodale Farms table at the Riverhead Farmers' Market.

If, like me, you have a "savory tooth" rather than a sweet tooth, you'll enjoy this dessert because it straddles that sweet-savory line. No, this dish does not taste at all like sauerkraut, but it does have a great texture courtesy of the noble cabbage.

Always ask your guests about their food allergies before serving them a dish, but never let on that there's sauerkraut in their dessert until after they've enjoyed it. —Stacy

SERVES 10 TO 12

1. Preheat the oven to 350°F. Butter two 9-inch cake pans. Line the bottoms of these pans with parchment paper and coat the parchment with cocoa powder. Line two additional 9-inch cake pans with parchment paper, but do not butter or powder them.

2. Coarsely chop the sauerkraut. Place the sauerkraut in the center of a cloth napkin, close the napkin around it and give it a squeeze to remove excess liquid.

3. In a stand mixer, cream the butter and sugar. Beat in the eggs and 1 teaspoon vanilla extract.

4. In a large mixing bowl, whisk together the cocoa powder, flour, baking soda, baking powder, and ¼ teaspoon salt. Mix the cocoa mixture, about a third at a time, into the butter mixture, alternating it with the stout and scraping down the beater and the sides of the mixer bowl, as needed. Stir in the sauerkraut.

5. Divide the batter evenly between the two lined cake pans that have been buttered and coated. Bake about 25 minutes, until the layers are springy and dry on top.

Continued . . .

FOR THE CAKE
10 tablespoons unsalted butter, at room temperature; additional butter for pan
½ cup unsweetened cocoa powder, more for pans
1 cup (8 ounces) packed sauerkraut, rinsed twice and thoroughly drained
1½ cups sugar
3 large eggs
1 teaspoon pure vanilla extract
2¼ cups all-purpose flour
1 teaspoon baking soda
1 teaspoon baking powder
¼ teaspoon fine sea salt
1 cup cream stout or strong coffee, at room temperature

FOR THE FILLING
1 vanilla pod
12 ounces cream cheese
3 tablespoons unsalted butter, at room temperature
¾ cup confectioners' sugar
2 tablespoons heavy whipping cream
¼ teaspoon pure vanilla extract
⅛ teaspoon fine sea salt

6. Cool the cake layers in the pans for about 15 minutes on a wire rack. Run a plastic knife around the edge of each layer. Invert each layer into a cake pan that has simply been lined with parchment paper. (This gives the layers very flat surfaces.) Place the cake layers in their new pans back on the wire rack to cool completely.

7. To make the filling, use a small, sharp knife to scrape the vanilla seeds from the vanilla pod into a clean stand mixer bowl. Add the cream cheese, 3 tablespoons butter, confectioners' sugar, 2 tablespoons cream, $\frac{1}{4}$ teaspoon vanilla extract and $\frac{1}{8}$ teaspoon salt and mix until smooth, about 1 minute, scraping down the sides of the bowl and the beater, as needed.

8. To make the glaze, melt 1 tablespoon butter in a small saucepan over low heat, and whisk in 1 tablespoon flour until blended. Gradually whisk in the $\frac{1}{4}$ cup cream. Cook, stirring constantly, until the mixture is thickened and smooth, about 3 minutes. Leave on the burner, but turn off the heat and stir in the whiskey, $\frac{1}{4}$ teaspoon vanilla extract, brown sugar, and $\frac{1}{8}$ teaspoon salt. Allow the glaze to cool for at least 30 minutes before applying it to the cake top.

9. To assemble the cake, remove the parchment paper from atop the cake layers. Center one cake layer on your serving dish. Remove the remaining parchment paper. Coat the cake layer evenly with half the filling. Center the other cake layer atop the filling. Remove the remaining parchment paper. Use the remaining half of the filling as frosting to thinly coat the sides and top of the cake. Slowly pour the glaze over the top layer of cake from its center outward, so that the top is completely covered and the glaze drips down the sides of the cake evenly. Give the glaze a few minutes to firm and then sprinkle finishing salt around the edge of the top of the cake. This cake may be served right away or chilled before serving.

STACY'S PAIRING: A sweet stout like Westhampton Beach Brewing Company Irish Eyes Cream Stout adds another layer of milk chocolate-like appeal when coupled with this cake, as its sweetness comes from lactose.

FOR THE GLAZE
1 tablespoon unsalted butter
1 tablespoon flour
$\frac{1}{4}$ cup heavy whipping cream
1 tablespoon corn whiskey
$\frac{1}{4}$ teaspoon pure vanilla extract
$\frac{3}{4}$ cup packed brown sugar
$\frac{1}{8}$ teaspoon fine sea salt
Amagansett Sea Salt or other finishing salt for garnish

Cider-Poached Apples on a Cloud of Cider-Sweetened Ricotta

FOR THE RICOTTA

1 cup whole milk ricotta cheese

¼ cup confectioners' sugar

¼ cup honey

1 teaspoon pure vanilla extract

½ cup heavy whipping cream, chilled

Ground cinnamon for garnish

FOR THE APPLES

4 Granny Smith apples

4 cups fresh apple cider

Juice of ½ lemon

¼ cup honey

I am convinced the Milk Pail Fresh Market in Water Mill makes the best cider ever known to man. Or to me. A half-gallon of their fresh pressed cider from their own apples, a paper cup, and a few of their homemade plain doughnuts is one of my pleasures, a guilty snack in the car and a warm-up before heading farther down the road to arduously gather pumpkins so big they could be used for Cinderella's coach. —Hillary

SERVES 4

1. Put the ricotta, sugar, ¼ cup honey, and vanilla in a food processor and process until smooth. Refrigerate until ready to use. Whip the cream until almost stiff and refrigerate until ready to use.

2. Peel and core the apples, slicing off just a bit on the bottom so they stand securely on their own.

3. Fill a saucepan big enough to hold the apples with the cider and lemon juice. Add the apples, bring to a simmer, and cook about 10 minutes, until the lower halves are tender but still holding their shape. Turn them over and cook another 10 minutes. Remove the apples to a colander and allow to cool to room temperature. Keep the poaching cider in the saucepan.

4. Measure out 3 cups of the poaching cider, transferring the rest to a bowl for another use. Pour the 3 cups back into the saucepan, bring to a boil, reduce to a simmer, pour in the ¼ cup honey, and cook at a vigorous simmer for 10 minutes to cook it down to about 1 cup of liquid. Take it off the heat.

5. To serve, gently fold the whipped cream into the ricotta, and divide this mixture onto the center of each plate. Top with an apple, and garnish with a light dusting of ground cinnamon. Ladle the apple syrup around the apples and serve.

STACY'S PAIRING: Wölffer Estate Vineyard Diosa Late Harvest is a white blend of Chardonnay, Pinot Gris, Vignoles, and Gewürztraminer, and it delivers the sweetness and depth of a grape-shaped cloud to accompany this honeyed dish.

Warm White Chocolate Parsnip Pudding

2 medium parsnips (about 8 ounces total), peeled and steamed until soft (about 15 minutes)

4 large eggs

2 cups heavy whipping cream

½ cup sugar

½ teaspoon pure vanilla extract

¼ teaspoon kosher salt

1 teaspoon grapeseed oil

4 ounces white baking chocolate

Ground ginger for sprinkling

This is what I might call a gateway parsnip dish. I would never claim that "even people who don't like parsnips like this dish." But certainly there are people who don't know what a parsnip tastes like and are parsnip curious. Parsnips are quite sweet and subtly earthy. Most people who have tried this dish, both the parsnip lovers and the parsnip questioning, ask for seconds. —Stacy

MAKES 6 PUDDINGS

1. Preheat the oven to 325°F.

2. Cut the cooked parsnips in half lengthwise and remove their cortexes (the tougher, inner roots) with a sharp paring knife. Place the parsnip pulp only in a food processor and process until pureed (it's okay if some chunks remain at this stage), about 30 seconds. Remove the parsnip pulp from the food processor and place it in the center of a cloth napkin. Fold the napkin closed and squeeze it to remove about 2 teaspoons of the juice. Place the squeezed pulp back into the food processor.

3. Place the eggs in a stand mixer and mix on low until they are lightly beaten, about 5 seconds. Add the cream, sugar, vanilla extract, and salt to the mixer bowl and mix until thoroughly combined, about 10 seconds.

4. Use a cup measure to remove about $\frac{1}{3}$ cup of the egg-cream mixture and place it in the food processor with the parsnip pulp. Process until the mixture is of a uniform consistency, about 10 seconds.

5. Stir the parsnip mixture into the egg-cream mixture in the mixer bowl.

6. Fill six 5-inch ramekins evenly with the mixture. Place the ramekins on a rimmed baking sheet. Place the baking sheet in the oven and bake until a thick, golden-brown crust has formed over the tops of the puddings, about 45 minutes. Remove the baking sheet from the oven and allow the custard to cool to room temperature.

7. Refrigerate the puddings until you are about ready to serve them. To serve, remove the puddings from the refrigerator and place all of the ramekins close together on a work surface.

8. Place the grapeseed oil and the white chocolate in a small saucepan over the lowest heat, stirring frequently. As soon as the chocolate has completely melted, use a small spoon to drizzle the chocolate mixture across the tops of the puddings. You may use a warm, damp cloth to wipe excess chocolate from the sides of the ramekins. I like to leave them messily arty. Sprinkle each pudding with a dash of ground ginger just before serving.

STACY'S PAIRING: A sweet Chardonnay with some character is called for—Castello di Borghese Vineyard Allegra Late Harvest Chardonnay melds with the white chocolate and the earthiness of the parsnips in this sweet dish.

APPENDIX: REUSE, RECYCLE, REJOICE!

Basic Stock

Oil for coating the pan

3 pounds poultry bones, backs, necks, and wing tips

1 pound onions or leeks (or onion, leek, shallot, and chive trimmings), whites and greens, roughly chopped

1 pound carrots (or carrot trimmings), roughly chopped

1 cup roughly chopped celery (or celery trimmings; optional)

2 tablespoons dry vermouth, such as Channing Daughters VerVino

2 tablespoons dried parsley or ¼ cup fresh carrot greens

1 teaspoon black peppercorns

1 teaspoon dried lovage or celery seed (optional)

2 bay leaves

6 quarts cold water

"Broth" is made from simmering meat, while "stock" is made from simmering bones. While it's true that stock can be made from whole vegetables and chickens, I really prefer spinning scraps into gold, both for the depth of flavor that using these seemingly ignoble ingredients brings and for the earth-motherly satisfaction of creating the culinary equivalent of rich compost.

I only use garlic and pepper scraps in stock that I know I'll be using for certain soups, like corn or pumpkin. But, if I'm honest, I don't use a recipe. Every Sunday, I just stuff roasted and cracked bones, vegetable trimmings, herbs, and peppercorns into a stockpot with some fresh water and wine and ignore it for a couple of hours. (Okay, true confession, I sometimes throw it all into a slow cooker and ignore it all night long, while the rising steam from the stock perfumes my dreams.)

This recipe gives you a good basic poultry stock. I advise not adding any salt until you're actually using the stock in a given dish, so you don't over-salt.

The thin, hollow bones of birds don't yield much more flavor beyond 2 hours of cooking, so if you choose to cook it longer, the stock will just be somewhat thicker. You can always thin it with some dry white wine. —Stacy

MAKES ABOUT 1 GALLON

1. Preheat the oven to 425°F.

2. Lightly coat a roasting pan with oil. Place all the bones and offcuts in a single layer in the roasting pan. Roast for about 30 minutes, until all are hot and sizzling. Remove the bones and pieces from the pan and place them on a large wooden cutting board.

3. Add just the larger pieces of vegetables (not the trimmings, if using) to the roasting pan and stir to coat them with some of the fat from the roasted bones. Roast the vegetables for about 15 minutes, until they are beginning to brown. Remove the roasting pan from the oven.

4. Meanwhile, cover the roasted bones with a kitchen towel and crack them by pounding them with a meat mallet. Place the bones in a large stockpot.

5. Add all the vegetables to the stockpot, along with the vermouth, parsley, peppercorns, lovage, and bay leaves. Add the cold water to the stockpot and place over medium-high heat until the mixture just starts to boil. Reduce the heat to medium-low and simmer, uncovered, for about 2 hours.

6. If you're not using the stock right away, strain it through a sieve into storage containers. Let the stock cool slightly, then refrigerate it.

7. After the stock has cooled, skim off any fat from the top. Use the refrigerated stock within 4 days or freeze it for up to 4 months.

If you make a beef or pork stock, you'll want to cook the stock for a minimum of three hours to unlock the bones' flavor. Fish stocks are more delicate and need only be simmered for about 30 minutes.

Compost

When I sat down to write a recipe for composting, I realized that I could write an entire book about my favorite part of the garden, my compost heap. But composting is dead simple. Carbon material—anything that has ever been alive—should not leave your property. Mother Nature takes otherwise useless items and transforms them into humus for your garden, or landscaping, free of charge.

It hit me that I could write everything you need to know for successful home composting in a recipe. So here it is. —*Stacy*

1. Site your compost heap in an area of lawn that's convenient to your kitchen door, avoiding extreme shade.

2. Use a shovel to remove the sod from the patch of land. Set the sod aside in a pile nearby, face down.

3. Line a bucket with a piece of newspaper and keep it in a handy spot on the floor of your kitchen. Place kitchen scraps and leftover cooking liquids in the lined bucket. Empty the bucket onto the prepared patch of land every time it fills, and before you go to bed at night, relining the bucket after each dumping.

4. About once a week, when you're dumping kitchen waste on the heap, toss on a chunk of the reserved sod as well.

5. About once a month, stab the compost heap all over with the shovel, about a dozen times, to aerate it.

6. After one year, use the shovel to remove the top layer from the heap, digging down until you reach compost that is uniformly dark and pliable. (Eggshells will still be visible—just crush them.) Apply this mature compost to your garden or to landscaping. Allow the newly placed compost to rest in situ for about 2 weeks before planting garden crops.

7. Place what was the top layer of compost back on the patch of land that you have now cleared of mature compost and start covering it with kitchen waste again.

4-foot-by-4-foot patch of land
Newspaper
Kitchen scraps (no bones, meat, fish, dairy, or soap)
Leftover cooking liquids
Grass and garden clippings (no mature weed or grass seeds)

STACY'S PAIRING: To make compost tea for watering microbes into your landscaping, place about 2 pounds of mature compost in an old tube sock, or pantyhose, and soak it in a 5-gallon bucket of water for 2 days, stirring occasionally. Remove the soaked compost from the sock and return it to the heap. Pour the tea into a watering can and use it within a few days. Don't drink this stuff!

Notes on Compost

- Don't be alarmed by the well-developed vermi-culture at work in your compost (so many worms!). That's all good.

- If something is edible, it's compostable. But certain foods like meat, fish, dairy, and cooked carbohydrates are magnets for vermin, so don't use them.

- If you have free-roaming dogs on your property, you must enclose your composting activities. Dogs are naturally drawn to rotting things, and immature compost is toxic to their digestive systems.

- If you have free-roaming chickens on your property, you can let them have full access to your composting. What they eat is turned into the only fertilizer richer than compost—manure. But be sure to remove any strings—such as teabag strings—from your kitchen waste before adding it to the heap. Strings can bind up a chicken internally and kill it.

- You can add manure and leaves to your compost heap for an even richer mix. The best common manures are chicken, sheep, goat, pig, cow, and horse. All manures must rest for at least one year before being placed in the garden.

- Be leery of neighbor's well-intentioned gifts of bags of leaves. Check them for excessive pet poop before layering them into your compost heap.

- Think of compost as pet food. You're mixing up a rich brew of goodies to attract as much healthy microflora and microfauna to your soil as possible. Applying compost is a way of building up your soil, year after year.

- A little salt, like the amount we use in cooking water, has no appreciable deleterious effect on composting. Certainly where I live, so close to the ocean, there are many salt-loving microbes in the natural environment.

- Rain and snow add nitrogen to the compost heap and settle it.

- Some items, such as disposable flatware and coffee pods, say they're "compostable" on their labels. This refers to composting in municipal systems where the temperature and pressure are much higher than in the home compost heap. These items won't break down in a year in a home compost heap. —Stacy

SEASONAL MENUS

Memorial Day Lunch by the Pool

Green Garlic Pesto Bites	(page 30)
Spring Onion and Arugula Salad with Yogurt Dressing	(page 32)
Hamptons Fish Burger with Microgreens	(page 38)
Traditional Strawberry Shortcake	(page 61)

Serve with a jubilant rosé like Wölffer Estate Vineyard Summer in a Bottle Rosé

Fourth of July Picnic

Mile-High Crustless Vegetable Pie	(page 72)
Beet-Stained Potato Salad with Chunky Scallions	(page 78)
Blue Cheese Chicken with Strawberry Salsa	(page 84)
Red Berry Pudding in Mason Jars	(page 94)

Serve with Wölffer Estate Vineyard Summer in a Bottle White Table Wine.

Labor Day Farewell Barbeque

Seared Tuna and Corn on the Cob	(pages 103 and 110)
BLT Macaroni Salad with Ham Crisps	(page 120)
Not-Your-Average Burger with Beer Cheese	(page 122)
Miracle Crust Peach-Berry Pie	(page 141)

Serve with Martha Clara Vineyards Syrah

Thanksgiving in Bridgehampton

Cod Mashed Potato Mini-Cakes	(page 152)
Caramelized Sweet Potato Slices	(page 154)
Savory Mushroom Bread Pudding	(page 156)
Green Salad with Roasted Cinnamon Bosc Pears	(page 163)
Heritage Turkey Breast	(page 176)
Long Island Cheese Pumpkin Pie	(page 180)
Farmhouse Apple Pie	(page 184)
East End Cheeseboard	(page 188)

Serve with Anthony Nappa Wines Bordo Antico

Winter Holiday Repast

Clam Chowder with Parsley Butter Croutons	(page 192)
Lettuce Boats with Swiss Cheese and Apples	(page 202)
Winter Storm Baked Fresh Ham with Mustard Sauce and Apple Chutney	(page 210)
Warm White Chocolate Parsnip Pudding	(page 228)

Serve with Martha Clara Vineyards Malbec Merlot

RESOURCES

We highly recommend a visit to the Hamptons. In the meantime, if you'd like to order some shippable Hamptons products for a taste of the good life, these purveyors may be able to work with you.

Amagansett Sea Salt Co.

This premium, unrefined finishing salt is crafted entirely by hand in small batches from the Atlantic Ocean. The traditional open-air process employs no chemicals or anticaking agents.

P.O. Box 1864, Amagansett, NY 11930
631-731-3053
amagansettseasalt.com

Bistro Été

Été means summer, but this popular Mediterranean-inspired French bistro is open all year, offering house-made cookies, dog biscuits, margarita mix, and more through their takeaway shop. Co-owner Arie Pavlou is the only Cyprus-born, Cordon Bleu–trained chef in the Hamptons.

760 Montauk Highway, Water Mill, NY 11976
631-500-9085
bistroete.com

Breadzilla

This cozy fixture of a hippie bakery in the woods creates an array of creative breads and desserts.

84 Wainscott Northwest Road, Wainscott, NY 11975
631-537-0955
breadzilla.com

Canio's Books

This independent bookstore offers new and used books, with an emphasis on East End–related books and signed editions.

290 Main Street, Sag Harbor, NY 11963
631-725-4926
canios.com

Carissa's the Bakery

Baker Carissa Waechter produces a wide variety of top-quality artisan breads, frequently using local grains and other local ingredients.

68 Newtown Lane, East Hampton, NY 11937
631-527-5996
carissasthebakery.com

Citarella Gourmet Markets

This New York–based chain arrived in the Hamptons in 1999. It brought the convenience of prepared foods and many specialty items in one store.

2209 Montauk Highway, Bridgehampton, NY 11932
2 Pantigo Road, East Hampton, NY 11937
20 Hampton Road, Southampton, NY 11968
631-283-6600
citarella.com

Fairview Farm at Mecox

Farmer Harry Ludlow and family promise sustainable, fresh, competitively priced local shopping made easy.

19 Horsemill Lane, Bridgehampton, NY 11932
631-537-6154
fairviewfarmatmecox.com

Good Water Farms

Farmer Brendan Davison grows a wide variety of colorful USDA/Northeast Organic Farming Association of New York–certified organic microgreens.

511 Mitchells Lane, Bridgehampton, NY 11932
631-604-1310
goodwaterfarms.com

HandcraftedHamptons.com

Southampton-based chef Bunnii Buglione creates some of the best artisan baked goods and handmade jams and jellies on the East End. She also curates a noteworthy collection of locally produced handicrafts. Production is so limited and seasonal that you'll want to peruse this website often.

Hildreth's

America's first department store offers a wide variety of indoor and outdoor furniture, housewares, and more, since 1842.

51 Main Street, Southampton, NY 11968
15 West Main Street, Southampton, NY 11968
109 Pantigo Road, East Hampton, NY 11937
1-800-INC-1842 (1-800-660-1842)
hildreths.com

L&W Market

This offshoot of Almond Restaurant offers prepared foods for takeout and a range of locally produced goods, including their popular line of condiments.

2493 Montauk Highway, Bridgehampton, NY 11932
631-537-1123
landwmarket.com

Loaves & Fishes Food Store

For more than 30 years, Loaves & Fishes Food Store has prepared gourmet takeout and catered food daily, from Easter week through New Year's Eve. Founded by food legend Anna Pump, the store is still family-owned and -operated.

50 Sagg Main Street, Sagaponack, NY 11962
631-537-0555
landffoodstore.com

Mecox Bay Dairy

Farmer Art Ludlow—and his herd of Jerseys—produce the Hamptons premier cow's milk cheeses, from firm to soft.

855 Mecox Road, Bridgehampton, NY 11932
631-537-0335
mecoxbaydairy.com

Milk Pail Fresh Market

This market offers their own apples, peaches, cider, and a range of other locally produced goods.

1346 Montauk Highway, Water Mill, NY 11976
631-537-2565
milk-pail.com

Montauk Brewing Company

New York State's easternmost brewery began as a basement brewing operation in 2012 among longtime friends. Montauk Brewing Company has grown to embody the spirit of Montauk—the come-as-you-are, no-frills good life, just steps from the surf.

62 South Erie Avenue, Montauk, NY 11954
631-668-8471
montaukbrewingco.com

Montauk Rumrunners

Crafted in honor of the families who once populated the historic Montauk Fishing Village and the real rumrunners among them, today's "rumrunners," sisters Kate Sarris and Kimberly Sarris Royal and their husbands, employ Long Island grains to produce their signature whiskey, gin, and vodka. All of their award-winning spirits are distributed throughout the Northeast.

montaukrumrunners.com

Open Minded Organics

Specializing in mushrooms, this farm stand offers a variety of organic and locally grown crops as well as prepared goods.

720 Butter Lane, Bridgehampton, NY 11932
631-255-0990
openmindedorganics.com

Round Swamp Farm

Both outlets of this glorified farm stand are bursting with a wide range of local produce and seafood, as well as packaged and prepared goods.

97 School Street, Bridgehampton, NY 11932
184 Three Mile Harbor Road, East Hampton, NY 11937
631-324-4438
roundswampfarm.com

Sag Harbor Rum

Old Whalers Style Sag Harbor Hand Crafted Rum's unique flavor is the result of being aged in old bourbon barrels and lightly infused with a blend of spices, fruits, and other natural flavors. This approach is inspired by the practice on whaling ships of storing rum in barrels that had previously been used for coffee, exotic spices, or fruit.

sagharborrum.com

Sagaponack Farm Distillery

The Sagaponack Farm Distillery on Sagg Road in Poxabogue sells its signature liquors (bourbon, rhubarb liqueur, rye, and whiskey) and the Foster family's Tiger Spuds Potato Chips through its tasting room. Its Sagaponacka Potato Vodka and Sagaponacka Wheat Vodka are also available in stores throughout the Hamptons.

369 Sagg Road, Sagaponack, NY 11962
sagaponackfarmdistillery.com

Southampton Publick House

Ranked as one of the top specialty breweries in the world, this local microbrewery sells its distinctive beers—IPAs, German-style beers, seasonal beers, and farmhouse ales—throughout the East Coast. You'll also find many of its beers on tap at its award-winning brewpub and at bars throughout Long Island.

62 Jobs Lane, Southampton, NY 11968
631-283-2800
publick.com

Wineries

Find the wineries of Long Island online.

liwines.com

ACKNOWLEDGMENTS

Part memoir, mostly cookbook, a bit of travelogue, and certainly an ode, *The Hamptons Kitchen* is the culmination of all that we love about living and dining in the Hamptons.

For my part, I wish first and foremost to thank my amazing coauthor, Stacy Dermont, for being a friend and enthusiastic companion food lover. This book would not have been possible without you.

To the ever insatiable Gael Greene, who wins me over every single time with her wit and big, good heart, and a hug, I give my utter gratitude for your enthusiasm and invaluable guidance. The world is a better place with you in it.

To our talented photographer, Barbara Lassen, thank you and thank you again for all the beautiful photographs, and for making our recipes come to life.

Thank you to our friend Barbara Barrielle for first introducing me to Stacy!

Special thanks go to Jane Dystel, our agent, for her encouragement and enthusiasm for this project.

To our editors, Róisín Cameron and Ann Treistman, and the entire team at The Countryman Press, thank you for giving us the chance to create the ultimate cookbook for the Hamptons.

Thanks to our tech team, graphic designer Joe Pallister and information specialist Lee Meyer.

To the many volunteers and friends who offer to test recipes, who have followed me from my previous cookbooks to this one, it's not possible to have enough words to express my gratitude. Those who went above and beyond for this book include Barbara Michelson, Sandy Sidwell, Kristy Stephens Ammann, Shelley Rashotsky, Eileen Mullen, Bonnie Elizabeth Chase, Lynda Phillipi, and Sarah Hodge, a huge thank you for your hard work. For your support, understanding, and encouragement, I would like to especially thank Angela Boyer-Stump, Shelby Coleman, Blandine Hafela, George Sheinberg, Hilda Longinotti, Shane Donahue, and Colleen Hildreth for the beautiful props she provided us from her family's store, Hildreth's Home Goods in Southampton.

Finally, my heart goes to James Barclay, who first introduced me to the Hamptons, who regaled me with its history, who shared his secret stops for local produce, and who was always willing to take a walk on the beach or cast a line out into the surf for dinner. Thank you for so graciously offering your home to our crew to shoot, for taste testing so many recipes, and for always offering to taste even more. With all my love, I dedicate this book to you. —*Hillary*

Gael Greene is my spirit animal. Edna Lewis is my patron saint. I dedicate all that I accomplish in this book to my dear friend and "fairy grandmother," the extraordinary journalist, novelist, and cookbook author Nancy Winters, whose guiding voice I still hear in my head. And, of course, to my actual grandmas, Arlene, Bessie, Elizabeth, and Mildred.

A number of communities inspired this work, including the Sunday Craftinate & Potluck Club at the home of artist Jeanelle Myers and Terry "the Performing Plumber" Sullivan; the Sag Harbor Farmers Market vendors and customers; the staffs and volunteers of many local nonprofit organizations including Chabad of Southhampton, Christ Episcopal Church, the Peconic Land Trust, the Sag Harbor Food Pantry, Slow Food East End, Stony Brook Southhampton Hospital, Sylvester Manor, and area historical societies.

Farmers Dale Haubrich and Bette Lacina were key to my understanding of what grows here and why, as was advice from local fisheries expert Al Daniels, with the avid support of his wife, Susan.

The legendary editor Susan Rafer took many a busman's holiday to offer her keen insights and encouragement. I hope I've made my writing teachers proud, especially Scott Chaskey, Jules Feiffer, Anabel Graff, Mr. Korthals, Robert Reeves, Roger Rosenblatt, and Gahan Wilson.

Thank you, for many and varied reasons to: Bobbie Cohen, Marilee Foster, Helen Harrison at the Pollock-Krasner House, Amelia Hundt, Chef Arie and Liz Pavlou, James Keith Phillips, and Maria Scotto.

And, always, we thank our local libraries, especially Penny Wright and her staff at the Rogers Memorial Library in Southampton and our welcoming audiences there, Catherine Creedon at the John Jermain Memorial Library in Sag Harbor, the gracious staff of the Hampton Library in Bridgehampton, and Maura Feeney at the Montauk Library.

And first in my heart, the family who puts up with my obsessions and recipe testing all of the time: Dan, Bo, and Angel. And to my parents Dr. Keith C. and Diane Carini; Tom and Kelly Dermont; Dr. Warren L. G. and Rebecca Koontz, who variously tested recipes and proofread and cheered me on.

Thank you to Blue Duck Bakery, Mecox Bay Dairy, Milk Pail Fresh Market, Open Minded Organics, Water Street Wines & Spirits, and retired farmer John Sidor Jr. for believing in this project so much that they insisted on donating some of their excellent produce and products.

All the other local produce and goods depicted were purchased from Amagansett Sea Salt, Balsam Farms, Browder's Birds, Country Gardens in Water Mill, the East Hampton Farmers Market, the Foster farm stand in Sagaponack, Good Water Farms, Pike Farms, the Southampton Farmers' Market, and the Springs Farmers' Market.

Many thanks to my recipe testers: Alison Althouse, Greg Barbera, Stacey Baum, Stephanie Bitis, Susan Blumenkrantz, Maria Cable, Kathy Camarata, Flora Cannon, Brian Cudzilo, Kaitlin Daniels, Laura Euler, Karen Grimes, Gen Horsburgh, Lynn Jacobsen, Lynda Judge, Larry Lewandowski, Oscar Mandes, and Julianne Melville.

All of the wines, beers, and liquors mentioned were purchased at their sources.

We encourage everyone to support their own local farmers and producers.

—Stacy

BIBLIOGRAPHY

To learn more about the food, and food culture, of the East End of Long Island, enjoy reading these books:

Chaskey, Scott. *Seedtime: On the History, Husbandry, Politics and Promise of Seeds,* 2014, New York: Rodale Books.

———. *This Common Ground: Seasons on an Organic Farm,* 2006, New York: Penguin Books.

Foster, Marilee. *Dirt Under My Nails: An American Farmer and Her Changing Land,* 2002, Bridgehampton, NY: Bridge Works Publishing.

Ladies' Village Improvement Society of East Hampton. *The 70th Anniversary Cookbook,* 1965, Southampton, NY: Southampton Press.

Lea, Robyn. *Dinner with Jackson Pollock,* 2014, New York: Assouline Publishing.

Pump, Anna and Sybille Pump with Gen LeRoy. *The Loaves and Fishes Party Cookbook,* 1990, New York: Harper & Row.

Starwood, Jane Taylor. *Long Island Wine Country,* 2009, Guilford, CT: Globe Pequot Press.

Villani, Stephanie and Kevin Bay. *The Fisherman's Wife: Sustainable Recipes and Salty Stories,* 2017, Wake Forest, NC: Breakwater Media.

INDEX

ABOUT THE AUTHORS

© Gavin Zeigler

Hillary Davis is the author of *Cuisine Niçoise*, *French Comfort Food*, *Le French Oven*, and *French Desserts*. She is a longtime food columnist and restaurant critic and has appeared on numerous television and radio programs. Her writing has been featured in *Connecticut Home Living*, *Hartford Magazine*, *Tastes of New England*, *The Boston Globe*, and other publications. Visit her online at Hillary-Davis.com.

© Barbara Lassen

Stacy Dermont is an Appalachian farm girl who was raised on homegrown produce, meat, and eggs. It was a natural fit for her to take over as a restaurant critic for *Dan's Papers*, "the Bible of the Hamptons," where she wrote over 2,000 "South o' the Highway" and "Hamptons Epicure" columns. She now spends most of her time in her Sag Harbor garden, plotting her next meal, and writing about local food and drink for *The Sag Harbor Express*.

MAY - 2020